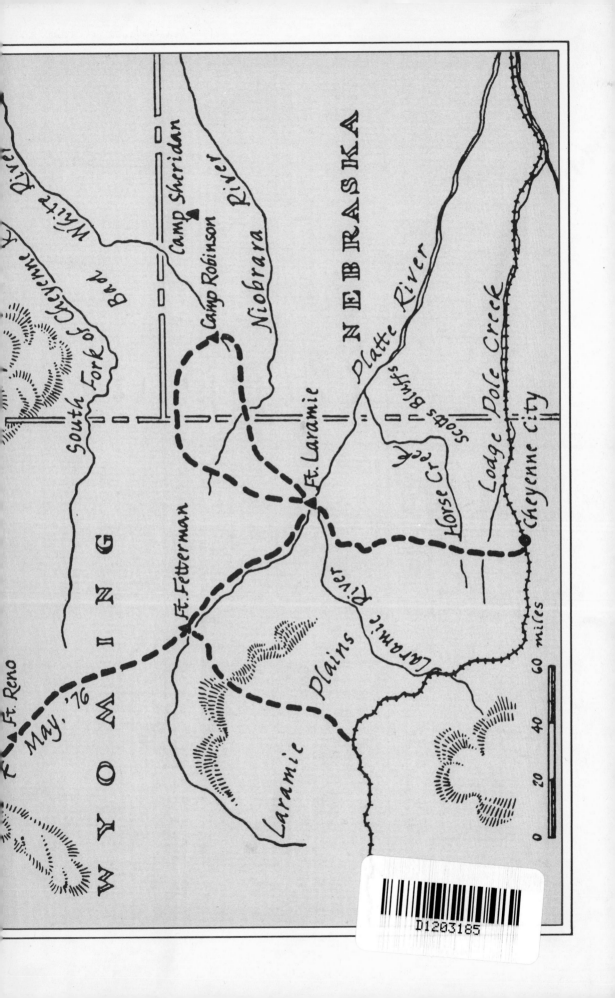

WYOMING

NEBRASKA

White River

Bad

South Fork of Cheyenne River

Camp Sheridan

Camp Robinson

Niobrara River

Platte River

Scotts Bluffs

Lodge Pole Creek

Horse Creek

Cheyenne City

Ft. Laramie

Ft. Fetterman

Laramie River

Laramie Plains

Ft. Reno

May '76

0   20   40   60 miles

AN ACCOUNT OF

CUSTER'S LAST CAMPAIGN

AND

THE BATTLE OF THE LITTLE BIG HORN,

BY

CAPTAIN E. S. GODFREY,

WHO COMMANDED CO. K

IN THE FIGHTING.

LEWIS OSBORNE: PALO ALTO, 1968

INTRODUCTION

THE FIRST BOOK to narrate and analyze the Battle of the Little Big Horn appeared within six months of the June day in 1876 when Lt. Col. George Armstrong Custer and some 250 officers and soldiers of the Seventh U.S. Cavalry perished in the most famous conflict of the Indian frontier. Since then the world's presses have poured forth a swelling stream of books, pamphlets and articles. The authoritative but incomplete Dustin bibliography listed 641 items as of 1953, and this ignored mountains of ephemera unworthy of inclusion in a bibliography. An updating could doubtless raise the total to no less than a thousand. In addition, Don Russell has cataloged more than 800 graphic representations of Custer's Last Stand ranging from the giant canvas of Edgar S. Paxson to a tiny portrayal on a milk-bottle cap. Motion pictures and television return to the theme time and time again.

The continuing flow of literature and art testifies to the continuing appeal of this clash of cavalry and Sioux on the remote Montana frontier. Surely one of the less significant episodes of the American past, it nevertheless combines elements of adventure, tragedy, suspense and mystery that save it from the obscurity of a footnote to history. A cast of complex, enigmatic characters endows it with a human interest the more engrossing because they are not fictional. In short, nearly any version of it makes a first-rate story.

For most of those who support the "Custeriana" market, a good story is enough. For a very great many, it is not. These are the "Custer buffs" who may be found in almost every corner of the world. (Dresden, East Germany, has boasted one of the finest museums anywhere of Little Big Horn *memorabilia*.) Infected by the Custer virus, the buffs digest every scrap of evidence, collate, analyze and synthesize, ponder the imponderable, seek answers to the unanswerable. Because the Custer Battle is freighted with more imponderables and more unanswerables than most events of the past, they guarantee that it will not recede from the national memory.

What manner of officers and men were the principals? the buffs want to know. They probe the personality and character of George A. Custer, flamboyant horseman with flowing yellow curls and gaudy uniforms, youthful boy-general of Civil War fame, hero of the Indian frontier, inspiring in others love or hate, admiration or contempt, rarely indifference; of Marcus A. Reno, colorless mediocrity, shadowed by misfortune, started toward self-destruction by the Little Big Horn; of Frederick W. Benteen, unsurpassed combat leader, embittered toward mankind, consumed with hatred for his commander; of Alfred H. Terry, kindly lawyer-turned-general; of John Gibbon, George Crook, and Philip Sheridan; of a regimental officer corps studded with individualists and divided into quarreling factions. What were their motivations, interrelationships, and roles in that campaign and battle?

How did it happen? Why did it happen? What precisely did happen? Who was to blame? Did Custer disobey orders? Or were Terry's orders permissive? What indeed did Terry intend? What did Custer intend? Did he blunder? Did Reno blunder? What was the sequence of movements on Custer Hill? Could Reno have saved Custer? If so, how? What if . . . ? On these and other hotly debated issues the buffs will never achieve consensus. But they will have fun trying.

For the would-be Custer buff, no better starting place can be found than Captain Godfrey's article in the January, 1892 issue of *The Century Magazine*, reprinted on the following pages. For the long-time student, few sources are more basic and indispensable. It comes from the pen of a literate participant with an authority drawn from personal observation reinforced by more than a

Major General George A. Custer, U. S. A.

decade of study, reflection, conversation with other participants, and a tour of the battlefield with some of the Indian leaders. It remains today the most accurate, least biased short account of the Little Big Horn campaign and battle.

The author, Capt. Edward S. Godfrey, was 49 years old in 1892 and a veteran of 25 years commissioned service, all in the Seventh Cavalry. Tall and lanky, his face marked by piercing eyes and a big nose from which depended one of the Army's most remarkable mustaches, he boasted an outstanding combat record on the Indian frontier. An 1867 graduate of West Point, Godfrey fought with Custer at the Washita in 1868 and marched with him on the Yellowstone Expedition of 1873 and the Black Hills Expedition of 1874. At the Little Big Horn he commanded Troop K in Benteen's battalion and served conspicuously in the defense of Reno Hill. At the Battle of Bear Paw Mountain, in the Nez Percé campaign of 1877, he further distinguished himself, received a severe wound, and later was rewarded with a Medal of Honor and a brevet of major. In 1890 he led his troop at the Battle of Wounded Knee, the last major engagement of the Indian Wars.

Viewing Godfrey's career, one is impressed with his stature as a thoroughly competent professional officer who resisted the frontier temptations that enervated or ruined so many of his contemporaries, and who held the respect and confidence of officers and soldiers alike. Of his associates, only Benteen has left any record of criticism of him, and he had good words for almost no one. Seniority rather than a superior record ultimately earned Godfrey promotion to field grade and finally, in 1907, to brigadier general. He retired in the same year. When he died in 1932 at the age of 88, only Col. Charles A. Varnum remained of the officers who rode with Custer to the Little Big Horn.

In 1876 Godfrey probably felt no particular animosity toward Major Reno or Captain Benteen and no particular partiality for

Custer. He was identified with neither the Custer nor the Benteen faction. By 1892 he had formed some biases that, despite a disciplined attempt at objectivity, show through in his *Century* article. His hostility to Reno is barely concealed. It seems to have emerged after the Battle of the Little Big Horn, when Reno was plunging into degradation and when Captain Benteen told him of Reno's proposal to abandon the wounded and withdraw from his hilltop position under cover of night.

Also evident in the *Century* article is a faint suggestion of pro-Custer bias. It probably reflects Godfrey's distaste for Reno more than a well-matured support of Custer. In later years, as he grew increasingly intimate with Custer's widow, Godfrey joined in her campaign to vindicate her husband and he became a more or less open Custer partisan. For this reason, his later writings have less value than the 1892 narrative.

The tinge of Custer bias in this account was greatly strengthened by association with the appended "remarks" of Gen. James B. Fry, a retired staff officer with a long list of publications on military topics to his credit. (Wrote Maj. James Brisbin* of Fry: "I presume there has been nothing since the birth of Christ that old Fry does not think he knows all about it.") Fry's remarks were

---

*Editor's note: Major Brisbin was a battalion commander in the column which reached the Little Big Horn on the day after the battle. His prior service on the plains and distinguished Civil War record, plus his opportunities to talk immediately with surviving soldiers, qualified him as an authority whose views are respected. General Fry, though never serving in the Indian Wars, also had a long and meritorious military career. His conclusions are valuable, though some scholars suggest that he was pro-Custer, in part, because both he and Custer were West Pointers. Brisbin was commissioned directly from civilian life in 1861. (Custer, Fry and Brisbin were all brevet Major-Generals after 1865, but at the time of the battle, Custer was serving as a Lieutenant-Colonel, Fry as a Colonel and Brisbin as a Major, their then-permanent ranking. As will be noted, however, Custer was usually addressed as "General" except in formal communications.)

frankly partisan and touched off a warm controversy in high military circles that lasted for more than a decade and that at one point made the commanding general of the Army party to a fabrication contrived to free Custer of the charge of disobeying orders.

During his long life Godfrey contributed enormously to the literature of the Custer Battle, not only directly through his own writings but indirectly through others whom he stimulated to write. But his 1892 article surpasses in value all his other contributions. It is fundamental to any study of the Little Big Horn for two reasons: it sets forth with precision, accuracy and brevity the basic facts of the campaign and battle; and it states or implies his opinions as a key participant and a reasonably dispassionate student on the basic questions in controversy. Amid the storms of verbiage that for nearly a century have obscured and confused the history of the Battle of the Little Big Horn, it has remained a beacon of clarity and authority.

Robert M. Utley

EDWARD S. GODFREY AS A 1ST LIEUTENANT, 7TH CAVALRY.

On the 16th of April, 1876, at McComb City, Missouri, I received orders to report my troop ("K," 7th Cavalry) to the Commanding General of the Department of Dakota, at St. Paul, Minnesota. At the latter place about twenty-five recruits fresh from civil life joined the troop, and we were ordered to proceed to Fort Abraham Lincoln, Dakota, where the Yellowstone Expedition was being organized. This expedition consisted of the 7th United States Cavalry, commanded by General George A. Custer, 28 officers and about 700 men; two companies of the 17th United States Infantry, and one company of the 6th United States Infantry, 8 officers and 135 men; one platoon of Gatling guns, 2 officers and 32 men (of the 20th United States Infantry); and 40 "Ree" Indian scouts. The expeditionary forces were commanded by Brigadier-General Alfred H. Terry, the Department Commander, who with his staff arrived several days prior to our departure.

On the 17th day of May, at 5 a.m., the "general"* was sounded, the wagons were packed and sent to the Quartermaster, and by six o'clock the wagon-train was on the road escorted by the infantry. By seven o'clock the 7th Cavalry was marching in column of platoon around the parade-ground of Fort Lincoln, headed by the band playing "Garry Owen," the Seventh's battle tune, first used when the regiment charged at the battle of Washita. The column was halted and dismounted just outside the garrison. The officers and married men were permitted to leave the ranks to say "good-by" to their families. General Terry, knowing the anxiety of the ladies, had assented to, or ordered, this demonstration, in order to allay their fears and satisfy them, by the formidable appearance we made, that we were able to cope with any enemy that we might expect to meet. Not many came out to witness the pageant, but many tear-filled eyes looked from the windows.

_____

* The signal to take down tents and break camp.

15

During this halt the wagon-train was assembled on the plateau west of the post and formed in column of fours. When it started off the "assembly" was sounded and absentees joined their commands. The signals "Mount" and "Forward" were sounded, and the regiment marched away, the band playing "The girl I left behind me."

The 7th Cavalry was divided into two columns, designated right and left wings, commanded by Major Marcus A. Reno and Captain F. W. Benteen. Each wing was subdivided into two battalions of three troops each. After the first day the following was the habitual order of march: one battalion was advance-guard, one was rear-guard, and one marched on each flank of the train. General Custer, with one troop of the advance-guard, went ahead and selected the route for the train and the camping-places at the end of the day's march. The other two troops of the advance-guard reported at headquarters for pioneer or fatigue duty, to build bridges and creek crossings. The rear-guard kept behind everything; when it came up to a wagon stalled in the mire, it helped to put the wagon forward. The battalions on the flanks were to keep within five hundred yards of the trail and not to get more than half a mile in advance or rear of the train. To avoid dismounting any oftener than necessary, the march was conducted as follows: one troop marched until about half a mile in advance of the train, when it was dismounted, the horses unbitted and allowed to graze until the train had passed and was about half a mile in advance of it, when it took up the march again; each of the other two troops would conduct their march in the same manner, so that two troops would be alongside the train all the time. If the country was much broken, a half dozen flankers were thrown out to guard against surprise. The flankers regulated their march so as to keep abreast of their troop. The pack-animals and beef herd were driven alongside the train by the packers and herders.

One wagon was assigned to each troop, and transported five days' rations and forage and the mess kit of the troop; also the mess kit, tents, and baggage of the troop officers and ten days' supplies for the officers' mess. The men were armed with the carbine and revolver; no one, not even the officer of the day, carried the saber. Each troop horse carried, in addition to the rider, between eighty and ninety pounds. This additional weight included all equipments and about one hundred rounds of ammunition. The wagon-train consisted in all of about one hundred and fifty wheeled vehicles. In it were carried thirty days' supplies of forage and rations (excepting beef), and two hundred rounds of ammunition per man. The two-horse wagons, hired by contract, carried from fifteen hundred to two thousand pounds. The six-mule government wagons carried from three to five thousand pounds, depending on the size and condition of the mules. The Gatling guns were each hauled by four condemned cavalry horses and marched in advance of the train. Two light wagons, loaded with axes, shovels, pickaxes and some pine boards and scantling, sufficient for a short bridge, accompanied the "pioneer" troops. The "crossings," as they are termed, were often very tedious and would frequently delay the train several hours. During this time the cavalry horses were unbitted and grazed, the men holding the reins. Those men not on duty at the crossing slept, or collected in groups to spin yarns and take a whiff at their "dingy dudeens." The officers usually collected near the crossing to watch progress, and passed the time in conversation and playing practical jokes. About noon the "strikers," who carried the haversacks, were called, and the different messes had their luncheon, sometimes separately, sometimes clubbing together. When the haversacks were opened, the horses usually stopped grazing and put their noses near their riders' faces and asked very plainly to share the hardtack; if their polite request did not receive attention they would paw the

ground, or even strike their riders. The old soldier was generally willing to share with his beast.

The length of the day's march, varying from ten to forty miles, was determined in a great measure by the difficulties or obstacles encountered, by wood, water, and grass, and by the distance in advance where such advantages were likely to be found. If, about two or three o'clock in the afternoon, a column of smoke was seen in the direction of the trail and a mile or two in advance, it was a pretty sure indication that a camp had been selected. The cavalry, excepting the rear-guard, would then cut loose from the train and go directly to camp. The rear-guard would send details to collect fuel and unpack their wagons. The adjutant showed the wing commanders the general direction their lines of tents were to run, and the latter then directed the battalion or troop commanders to their camping-places. Generally one flank of each line would rest near the creek. The general form of the camp was that of a parallelogram. The wings camped on the long sides facing each other, and the headquarters and guard were located at one end nearest to the creek; the wagon-train was parked to close the other end and was guarded by the infantry battalion. The troops, as they arrived at their places, were formed in line, facing inward, dismounted, unsaddled, and, if the weather was hot and the sun shining, the men rubbed the horses' backs until dry. After this the horses were sent to water and put out to graze, with side-lines and lariats, under charge of the stable guard, consisting of one non-commissioned officer and three or six privates. The men of the troop then collected fuel, sometimes wood, often a mile or more distant from the camp; sometimes "buffalo chips." The main guard, consisting, usually, of four or five non-commissioned officers and twelve or fifteen privates, reported mounted at headquarters, and were directed to take posts on prominent points overlooking the camp and surrounding country, to guard against surprise. Each post consisted of one non-commissioned officer and three privates. The officer of the day, in addition to his ordinary duties in camp, had charge of the safety of the cavalry herds. Sometimes this latter duty was performed by an officer designated as "Officer of the Herd." To preserve the grazing in the immediate vicinity of the camp for evening and night grazing, all horses were required to be outside of the camp limits until retreat. When the train arrived, the headquarters and troop wagons went directly to the camping-place of their respective commands. The officers'

baggage and tents were unloaded first; then the wagons went near the place where the troop kitchen was to be located, always on that flank of the troop farthest from headquarters. The teamsters unharnessed their mules and put them out to graze. The old stable guard reported to the troop commander for fatigue duty to put up the officers' tents and collect fuel for their mess. The troop officers' tents were usually placed twenty-five yards in rear of the line of men's tents and facing toward them. Their cook or mess tent was placed about ten or fifteen yards further to the rear. The "striker" made down the beds and arranged the "furniture," so to speak, which generally consisted of a camp-stool, tin wash-basin, and a looking glass. The men put up their tents soon after caring for their horses. The fronts of their tents were placed on a line established by stretching a picket-rope. The first sergeant's was on that flank of the line nearest to the headquarters. The horse equipments were placed on a line three yards in front of the tents. The men were not prohibited from using their saddles as pillows. A trench was dug for the mess fire, and the grass was burned around it for several yards to prevent prairie fires. After this the cooks busied themselves preparing supper. Beef was issued soon after the wagon-train came in, and the necessary number of beeves were butchered for the next day's issue; this was hauled in the wagons. Stable call was sounded about an hour before sunset.

The men of each troop were formed on the parade and marched to the horse herds by the first sergeant. Each man went to his own horse, took off the side-lines and fastened them around the horse's neck, then pulled the picket-pin, coiled the lariat, noosed the end fastened to the head halter around the horse's muzzle, mounted, and assembled in line at a place indicated by the first sergeant. The troop was then marched to the watering-place, which was usually selected with great care because of the boggy banks and miry beds of the prairie streams. After watering, the horses were lariated outside but in the immediate vicinity of the camp. The ground directly in rear of the troop belonged to it, and was jealously guarded by those concerned against encroachment by others. After lariating their horses, the men got their curry-combs, brushes, and nose-bags, and went to the troop wagon, where the quartermaster-sergeant and farrier measured, with tin cups, the forage to each man, each watching jealously that he got as much for his horse as those before him. He then went at once to feed and groom his horse. The officer whose duty it was to attend stables and the first sergeant superintended the grooming, examining each horse's back and feet carefully to see if they were all right. When a horse's back got sore through the carelessness of the rider, the man would generally be compelled to lead his horse until the sore was well. Immediately after stables, the cooks announced in a loud tone "supper." The men with haversack and tin cup went to the mess fire and got their hardtack, meat, and coffee. If game had been killed the men did a little extra cooking themselves.

The troop officers' mess kits consisted of a sheet-iron cooking-stove, an iron kettle, stewing, frying, baking, and dish pans; a a small Dutch oven, a camp-kettle, a mess-chest holding tableware for four persons, and a small folding-table. The table in fair weather was spread in the open air. The early part of the meal was a matter of business, but after the substantials were stowed away, the delicacies were eaten more leisurely and time found for conversation. After supper the pipes were lighted, and the officers, if the weather was cold, went to the windward side of the campfire. Each man as he took his place was sure to poke or kick the fire, turn his back, hitch up his coat-tail, and fold his hands behind him.

Retreat was sounded a little after sunset and the roll was called, as much to insure the men having their equipments in place as to secure their presence, for it was not often we were near enough to any attraction to call the men away. (In 1876 there was not a ranch west of Bismarck, Dakota, nor east of Bozeman, Montana.) The stable guards began their tours of duty at this time. The non-commissioned officer reported to the troop commander for instructions for the night; these usually designated whether the horses were to be tied to the picket-line or kept out to graze, and included special instructions for the care of sick or weak horses. At dusk all horses were brought within the limits of the camp. The picket-line was stretched over three wagons in front of the men's tents, or three posts were used when remaining in camp over a day.

During the evening the men grouped about the fires and sang songs and spun yarns until "taps." The cooks prepared the breakfast, which usually consisted of hard bread, bacon, and coffee. If beans or fresh meat were to be cooked, the food was put into the Dutch ovens or camp-kettles, which were placed in the fire trench, covered over with hot ashes and coals, and a fire built over them. If the wind blew hard all fires were extinguished, to prevent prairie fires. The cooks were called an hour or an hour and a half before reveille. At the first call for reveille, usually 4:20 a.m., the stable guard awakened the occupants of each tent and the officer whose duty it was to attend the roll-call. Stable call followed reveille and was superintended by an officer. This occupied

TROOPERS SADDLING THEIR MOUNTS I

PREPARATION FOR THE DAY'S MARCH.

about three-quarters of an hour. Two hours after reveille, the command would be on the march. Of course there were incidents that occasionally relieved the monotony.

Antelope were very plentiful, and the men were encouraged by troop commanders to hunt. General Custer had a number of stag-hounds, which amused themselves and the command in their futile attempts to catch them. One morning they started up a large buck near where the column was marching; Lieutenant Hare immediately followed the hounds, passed them, drew his revolver, and shot the buck. Nothing of special interest occurred until the 27th of May, when we came to the Bad Lands of the Little Missouri River. On the 30th General Custer was sent with four troops to make a scout up the Little Missouri, for about twenty miles. He returned the same day, without having discovered any recent "Indian signs." On the 31st we crossed the Little Missouri without difficulty. On the 1st and 2d of June we were obliged to remain in camp on account of a snow-storm.

We remained in camp on the Powder River for three days. General Terry went to the Yellowstone to communicate with the supply steamer *Far West*, which was at the mouth of the Powder River. He also went up the Yellowstone to communicate with General Gibbon's command, known as the "Montana Column," composed of four troops of the 2d Cavalry and several companies of the 7th Infantry. Before General Terry left it was given out that the 7th Cavalry would be sent to scout up the Powder River, while the wagon-train, escorted by the infantry, would be sent to establish a supply camp at the mouth of the Powder.

Eleven pack-mules, saddles, and aparejos were issued to each troop for this scout. This was a new departure; neither officers, men, nor mules had had any experience with this method of transportation. There were a few "packers" (civilian employés) to give instructions. Short, compactly built mules, the best for the purpose, were selected from the teams. A non-commissioned officer and four men of each troop were detailed for packers. After some instruction had been given by the professionals, especially how to tie the "diamond hitch," we concluded to make our maiden attempt by packing two empty water-casks. The mule was blinded and he submitted, with some uneasiness, to the packing. We supposed the packs were securely fastened and did not anticipate any trouble; but it is always the unexpected that happens with a mule. The blind was lifted; the mule gave a startled look first to one side, then to the other, at the two casks bandaged to his sides. He jumped to one side, causing to rattle a bung-plug that had fallen inside one of the casks. This startled him still more, and with head and tail high in the air he jumped again. He snorted and brayed, bucked and kicked, until the casks fell off. One was fastened to the saddle by the sling-rope. He now began to run, braying and making such a "rumpus" that the camp turned out as spectators. The affair excited serious concern lest all the animals in camp would be stampeded. When the cask was loose we got him back and made a second attempt with two sacks of grain. These he soon bucked off and then regaled himself with the spilt grain. As a final effort we concluded to try the aparejo, and pack two boxes of ammunition. This done, the mule walked off with as little concern as if he had been a pack-mule all his life.

General Terry having returned, orders were issued on the 10th for the right wing, six troops, under Major Reno, to make a scout up the Powder, provided with twelve days' rations.

The left wing was ordered to turn over all forage and rations; also the pack-mules, except four to each troop. Major Reno left at 3 p.m., and the next day the rest of the command marched to the mouth of the Powder. My troop was rear-guard, and at times we were over three miles in rear of the wagon-train waiting on the packers, for we had taken this opportunity to give them practical instruction.

Up to this time we had not seen an Indian, nor any recent signs of them, except one small trail of perhaps a half dozen tepees, evidently of a party of agency Indians on their way to join the hostile camps. The buffalo had all gone west; other game was scarce and wild. Indications were that the Indians were west of the Powder, and information from General Gibbon placed them south of the Yellowstone. Some officers of the right wing before they left expressed their belief that we would not find any Indians, and were sanguine that we would all get home by the middle of August.

Major Reno was ordered to scout to the forks of the Powder, then across to Mizpah Creek, follow it down to near its confluence with the Powder; then cross over to Pumpkin Creek, follow it down to the Tongue River, scout up that stream, and then rejoin the regiment at the mouth of the Tongue by the time his supplies were exhausted; unless, in the mean time, he should make some discovery that made it necessary to return sooner to make preparations for pursuit. A supply depot was established at the mouth of the Powder, guarded by the infantry, at which the wagon-train was left.

General Terry, with his staff and some supplies, took passage on the supply steamer *Far West*, and went up to the mouth of the Tongue. General Custer, with the left wing, marched to the mouth of the Tongue, where we remained until the 19th waiting tidings from Reno's scout. The grounds where we camped had been occupied by the Indians the previous winter. (Miles City, Montana, was first built on the site of this camp.) The rude shelters for their ponies, built of driftwood, were still standing and furnished fuel for our camp-fires. A number of their dead, placed upon scaffolds, or tied to the branches of trees, were disturbed and robbed of their trinkets. Several persons rode about exhibiting trinkets with as much gusto as if they were trophies of their valor, and showed no more concern for their desecration than if they had won them at a raffle. Ten days later I saw the bodies of these same persons dead, naked, and mutilated.

On the 19th of June tidings came from Reno that he had found a large trail that led up the Rosebud River. The particulars were not generally known. The camp was full of rumors; credulity was raised to the highest pitch, and we were filled with anxiety and curiosity until we reached Reno's command, and learned the details of their discoveries. They had found a large trail on the Tongue River, and had followed it up the Rosebud about forty miles. The number of lodges in the deserted villages was estimated by the number of camp-fires remaining to be about three hundred and fifty. The indications were that the trail was about three weeks old. No Indians had been seen, nor any recent signs. It is not probable that Reno's movements were known to the Indians, for on the very day Reno reached his farthest point up the Rosebud, the battle of the Rosebud, between General Crook's forces and the Indians, was fought. The two commands were then not more than forty miles apart, but neither knew nor even suspected the proximity of the other.

We reached the mouth of the Rosebud about noon on the 21st, and began preparations for the march and the battle of the Little Big Horn.

There were a number of Sioux Indians who never went to an agency except to visit friends and relatives. They camped in and roamed about the Buffalo Country. Their camp was the rendezvous for the agency Indians when they went out for their annual hunts for meat and robes. They were known as the "Hostiles," and comprised representatives from all the different tribes of the Sioux nation. Many of them were renegade outlaws from the agencies. In their visits to the agencies they were usually arrogant and fomenters of discord. Depredations had been made upon the

GENERAL GIBBON

SITTING BULL

commerce to the Black Hills, and a number of lives taken by them or by others, for which they were blamed. The authorities at Washington had determined to compel these Indians to reside at the agencies — hence the Sioux War. Sitting Bull, an Uncpapa Sioux Indian, was the chief of the hostile camp; he had about sixty lodges of followers on whom he could at all times depend. He was the host of the Hostiles, and as such received and entertained their visitors. These visitors gave him many presents, and he was thus enabled to make many presents in return. All visitors paid tribute to him, so he gave liberally to the most influential, the chiefs, *i. e.,* he "put it where it would do the most good." In this way he became known as the chief of the hostile Indian camp, and the camp was generally known as "Sitting Bull's camp." Sitting Bull was a heavy-set, muscular man, about five feet eight inches in stature, and at the time of the battle of the Little Big Horn was forty-two years of age. He was the autocrat of the camp — chiefly because he was the host. In council his views had great weight, because he was known as a great medicine man. He was a chief, but not a warrior chief. In the war councils he had a voice and vote the same as any other chief. A short time previous to the battle he had "made medicine," had predicted that the soldiers would attack them and that the soldiers would all be killed. He took no active part in the battle, but, as was his custom in time of danger, remained in the village "making medicine." Personally he was regarded as a great coward and a very great liar, "a man with a big head and a little heart." The command passed the remains of a "Sundance" lodge which took place about June 5, and to which I shall again refer. This was always a ceremony of great importance to the Indians. It ranks in interest and importance to the Indians with the graduation or commencement exercises of our civilized communities. In anticipation of this event, the Indians from the agencies had assembled at this camp.

Major James McLaughlin, United States Indian Agent, stationed at the Devil's Lake Agency, Dakota, from 1870 to 1881, and at Standing Rock Agency, Dakota, from 1881 to the present time, has made it a point to get estimates of the number of Indians at the hostile camp at the time of the battle. In his opinion, and all who know him will accept it with confidence, about one-third of the whole Sioux nation, including the northern Cheyennes and Arapahoes, were present at the battle; he estimates the number present as between twelve and fifteen thousand; that one out of four is a low estimate in determining the number of warriors present; every male over fourteen years of age may be considered a warrior in a general fight such as was the battle of the Little Big Horn; also, considering the extra hazards of the hunt and expected battle, fewer squaws would accompany the recruits from the agencies. The minimum strength of their fighting men may then be put down as between twenty-five hundred and three thousand. Information was despatched from General Sheridan that from one agency alone about eighteen hundred lodges had set out to join the hostile camp; but that information did not reach General Terry until several days after the battle. The principal warrior chiefs of the hostile Indians were: "Gall," "Crow King," and "Black Moon," Uncpapa Sioux; "Low Dog," "Crazy Horse," and "Big Road," Ogalla Sioux; "Spotted Eagle," Sans-Arc Sioux; "Hump" of the Minneconjous; and "White Bull" and "Little Horse," of the Cheyennes. To these belong the chief honors of conducting the battle, of whom, however, "Gall," "Crow King," and "Crazy Horse" were the ruling spirits.

Generals Terry, Gibbon, and Custer had a conference on board the steamer *Far West*. It was decided that the 7th Cavalry, under General Custer, should follow the trail discovered by Reno. "Officers' call" was sounded as soon as the conference had concluded. Upon assembling, General Custer gave us our orders. We

CROW KING

were to transport on our pack-mules fifteen days' rations of hard bread, coffee, and sugar; twelve days' rations of bacon, and fifty rounds of carbine ammunition per man. Each man was to be supplied with 100 rounds of carbine and 24 rounds of pistol ammunition, to be carried on his person and in his saddle-bags. Each man was to carry on his horse twelve pounds of oats. The pack-mules sent out with Reno's command were badly used up, and promised seriously to embarrass the expedition. General Custer recommended that some extra forage be carried on the pack-mules. In endeavoring to carry out this recommendation some troop commanders foresaw the difficulties, and told the General that some of the mules would certainly break down, especially if the extra forage was packed. He replied in an excited manner, quite unusual with him: "Well, gentlemen, you may carry what supplies you please; you will be held responsible for your companies. The extra forage was only a suggestion, but this fact bear in mind, we will follow the trail for fifteen days unless we catch them before that time expires, no matter how far it may take us from our base of supplies; we may not see the supply steamer again;" and, turning as he was about to enter his tent, he added, "You had better carry along an extra supply of salt; we may have to live on horse meat before we get through." He was taken at his word, and an extra supply of salt was carried. "Battalion" and "wing" organizations were broken up, and troop commanders were responsible only to General Custer. His written instructions were as follows:

CAMP AT MOUTH OF ROSEBUD RIVER, MONTANA TERRITORY, June 22d, 1876. LIEUTENANT-COLONEL CUSTER, 7TH CAVALRY. COLONEL: The Brigadier-General Commanding directs that, as soon as your regiment can be made ready for the march, you will proceed up the Rosebud in pursuit of the Indians whose trail was discovered by Major Reno a few days since. It is, of course, impossible to give you any definite instructions in regard to this movement, and were it not impossible to do so the Department Commander places too much confidence in your zeal, energy, and ability to wish to impose upon you precise orders which might hamper your action when nearly in contact with the enemy. He will, however, indicate to you his own views of what your action should be, and he desires that you should conform to them unless you shall see sufficient reason for departing from them. He thinks that you should proceed up the Rosebud until you ascertain definitely the direction in which the trail above spoken of leads. Should it be found (as it appears almost certain that it will be found) to turn towards the Little Horn, he thinks that you should still proceed southward, perhaps as far as the headwaters of the Tongue, and then turn towards the Little Horn, feeling constantly, however, to your left, so as to preclude the possibility of the escape of the Indians to the south or southeast by passing around your left flank. The column of Colonel Gibbon is now in motion for the mouth of the Big Horn. As soon as it reaches that point it will cross the Yellowstone and move up at least as far as the forks of the Big and Little Horns. Of course its future movements must be controlled by circumstances as they arise, but it is hoped that the Indians, if upon the Little Horn, may be so nearly inclosed by the two columns that their escape will be impossible.

The Department Commander desires that on your way up the Rosebud you should thoroughly examine the upper part of Tulloch's Creek, and that you should endeavor to send a scout through to Colonel Gibbon's column, with information of the result of your examination. The lower part of this creek will be examined by a detachment from Colonel Gibbon's command. The supply steamer will be pushed up the Big Horn as far as the forks if the river is found to be navigable for that distance, and the Department Commander, who will accompany the column of Colonel Gibbon, desires you to report to him there not later than the expiration of the time for which your troops are rationed, unless in the mean time you receive further orders. Very respectfully, your obedient servant, E. W. SMITH, Captain 18th Infantry, Acting Assistant Adjutant-General.

These instructions are explicit, and fixed the location of the Indians very accurately. Of course as soon as it was determined that we were to go out, nearly every one took time to write letters home, but I doubt very much if there were many of a cheerful nature. Some officers made their wills; others gave verbal instructions as to the disposition of personal property and distribution of mementos; they seemed to have a presentiment of their fate.

At twelve o'clock, noon, on the 22d of June, the "Forward" was sounded, and the regiment marched out of camp in column of fours, each troop followed by its pack-mules. Generals Terry, Gibbon, and Custer stationed themselves near our line of march and reviewed the regiment. General Terry had a pleasant word for each officer as he returned the salute. Our pack-trains proved troublesome at the start, as the cargoes began falling off before we got out of camp, and during all that day the mules straggled badly. After that day, however, they were placed under the charge of an officer, who was directed to report at the end of each day's march the order of merit of the efficiency of the troop packers. Doubtless General Custer had some ulterior design in this. It is quite probable that if he had had occasion to detach troops requiring rapid marching, he would have selected those whose packers had the best records. At all events the efficiency was much increased, and after we struck the Indian trail the pack-trains kept well closed.

We went into camp about 4 p.m., having marched twelve miles. About sunset "officers' call" was sounded, and we assembled at General Custer's bivouac and squatted in groups about the General's bed. It was not a cheerful assemblage; everybody seemed to be in a serious mood, and the little conversation carried on, be-

CUSTER IN THE BUCKSKINS HE WORE DURING THE CAMPAIGN.

fore all had arrived, was in undertones. When all had assembled
the General said that until further orders trumpet-calls would
not be sounded except in an emergency; the marches would begin
at 5 a.m. sharp; the troop commanders were all experienced officers, and knew well enough what to do, and when to do what was
necessary for their troops; there were two things that would be
regulated from his headquarters, *i.e.,* when to move out of and
when to go into camp. All other details, such as reveille, stables,
watering, halting, grazing, etc., on the march would be left to the
judgment and discretion of the troop commanders; they were to
keep within supporting distance of each other, not to get ahead of
the scouts, or very far to the rear of the column. He took particular pains to impress upon the officers his reliance upon their judgment, discretion, and loyalty. He thought, judging from the
number of lodge-fires reported by Reno, that we might meet at
least a thousand warriors; there might be enough young men
from the agencies, visiting their hostile friends, to make a total
of fifteen hundred. He had consulted the reports of the Commis-
sioner of Indian Affairs as to the probable number of "Hostiles"
(those who had persistently refused to live or enroll themselves
at the Indian agencies), and he was confident, if any reliance was
to be placed upon those reports, that there would not be an opposing force of more than fifteen hundred. General Terry had of-
fered him the additional force of the battalion of the 2d Cavalry,
but he had declined it because he felt sure that the 7th Cavalry
could whip any force that would be able to combine against him;
that if the regiment could not, no other regiment in the service
could; if they could whip the regiment, they would be able to defeat a much larger force, or, in other words, the reinforcement of
this battalion could not save us from defeat. With the regiment
acting alone there would be harmony, but another organization
would be sure to cause jealousy. He had declined the offer of the

Gatling guns for the reason that they might hamper our movements or march at a critical moment, because of the difficult nature of the country through which we would march. The marches would be from twenty-five to thirty miles a day. Troop officers were cautioned to husband their rations and the strength of their mules and horses, as we might be out for a great deal longer time than that for which we were rationed, as he intended to follow the trail until we could get the Indians, even if it took us to the Indian agencies on the Missouri River or in Nebraska. All officers were requested to make to him, then or at any time, any suggestions they thought fit.

This "talk" of his, as we called it, was considered at the time as something extraordinary for General Custer, for it was not his habit to unbosom himself to his officers. In it he showed a lack of self-confidence, a reliance on somebody else; there was an indefinable something that was not Custer. His manner and tone, usually brusque and aggressive, or somewhat rasping, was on this occasion conciliating and subdued. There was something akin to an appeal, as if depressed, that made a deep impression on all present. We compared watches to get the official time, and separated to attend to our various duties. Lieutenants McIntosh, Wallace,* and myself walked to our bivouac, for some distance in silence, when Wallace remarked: "Godfrey, I believe General Custer is going to be killed." "Why, Wallace," I replied, "what makes you think so?" "Because," said he, "I have never heard Custer talk in that way before."

I went to my troop and gave orders what time the "silent" reveille should be and as to other details for the morning preparations; also the following directions in case of a night attack: the stable guard, packers, and cooks were to go out at once to the

---

*Killed at the battle of Wounded Knee, December 29, 1890.

horses and mules to quiet and guard them; the other men were to go at once to a designated rendezvous and await orders; no man should fire a shot until he received orders from an officer to do so. When they retired for the night they should put their arms and equipments where they could get them without leaving their beds. I then went through the herd to satisfy myself as to the security of the animals. During the performance of this duty I came to the bivouac of the Indian scouts. "Mitch" Bouyer, the half-breed interpreter, "Bloody Knife," the chief of the Ree scouts, "Half-Yellow-Face," the chief of the Crow scouts, and others were having a "talk." I observed them for a few minutes, when Bouyer turned toward me, apparently at the suggestion of "Half-Yellow-Face," and said, "Have you ever fought against these Sioux?" "Yes," I replied. Then he asked, "Well, how many do you expect to find?" I answered, "It is said we may find between one thousand and fifteen hundred." "Well, do you think we can whip that many?" "Oh, yes, I guess so." After he had interpreted our conversation, he said to me with a good deal of emphasis, "Well, I can tell you we are going to have a —— big fight."

At five o'clock, sharp, on the morning of the 23d, General Custer mounted and started up the Rosebud, followed by two sergeants, one carrying the regimental standard and the other his personal or headquarters flag, the same kind of flag as used while commanding his cavalry division during the Rebellion. This was the signal for the command to mount and take up the march. Eight miles out we came to the first of the Indian camping-places. It certainly indicated a large village and numerous population. There were a great many "wickiups" (bushes stuck in the ground with the tops drawn together, over which they placed canvas or blankets). These we supposed at the time were for the dogs, but subsequent events developed the fact that they were the temporary shelters of the transients from the agencies. During the day we passed through three of these camping-places and made halts at each one. Everybody was busy studying the age of pony droppings and tracks and lodge trails, and endeavoring to determine the number of lodges. These points were the all-absorbing topics of conversation. We went into camp about five o'clock, having marched about thirty-three miles.

June 24th we passed a great many camping-places, all appearing to be of nearly the same strength. One would naturally suppose these were the successive camping-places of the same village, when in fact they were the continuous camps of the several bands. The fact that they appeared to be of nearly the same age, that is, having been made at the same time, did not impress us then. We passed through one much larger than any of the others. The grass for a considerable distance around it had been cropped close, indicating that large herds had been grazed there. The frame of a large "Sun-dance" lodge was standing, and in it we found the scalp of a white man, probably one of General Gibbon's command who had been killed some weeks previously. It was whilst here that the Indians from the agencies had joined the Hostiles' camp. The command halted here and "officers' call" was sounded. Upon assembling we were informed that our Crow scouts, who had been very active and efficient, had discovered fresh signs, the tracks of three or four ponies and of one Indian on foot. At this time a stiff southerly breeze was blowing; as we were about to separate, the General's headquarters flag was blown down, falling to our rear. Being near the flag, I picked it up and stuck the staff in the ground, but it fell again to the rear. I then bored the staff into the ground where it would have the support of a sage-bush. This circumstance made no impression on me at the time, but after the battle an officer asked if I remembered the incident; he had observed it, and regarded the fact of its falling to the rear as a bad omen, and felt sure we would suffer a defeat.

The march during the day was tedious. We made many long halts so as not to get ahead of the scouts, who seemed to be doing their work thoroughly, giving special attention to the right, toward Tulloch's Creek, the valley of which was in general view from the divide. Once or twice signal smokes were reported in that direction. The weather was dry and had been for some time, consequently the trail was very dusty. The troops were required to march on separate trails so that the dust clouds would not rise so high. The valley was heavily marked with lodge-pole trails and pony tracks, showing that immense herds of ponies had been driven over it. About sundown we went into camp under the cover of a bluff, so as to hide the command as much as possible. We had marched about twenty-eight miles. The fires were ordered to be put out as soon as supper was over, and we were to be in readiness to march again at 11:30 p.m. Lieutenant Hare and myself lay down about 9:30 to take a nap; when comfortably fixed we heard some one say, "He's over there by that tree." As that described our locality pretty well, I called out to know what was wanted, and the reply came: "The General's compliments and wants to see all the officers at headquarters immediately." So we gave up our much-needed rest and groped our way through horse herds, over sleeping men, and through thickets of bushes trying to find headquarters. No one could tell us, and as all fires and lights were out we could not keep our bearings. We finally espied a solitary candle-light, toward which we traveled, and found most of the officers assembled at the General's bivouac. The General said that the trail led over the divide to the Little Big Horn; the march would be taken up at once, as he was anxious to get as near the divide as possible before daylight, where the command would be concealed during the day, and give ample time for the country to be studied, to locate the village and to make plans for the attack on the 26th. We then returned to our troops, except Lieutenant

Hare, who was put on duty with the scouts. Because of the dust it was impossible to see any distance, and the rattle of equipments and clattering of the horses' feet made it difficult to hear distinctly beyond our immediate surroundings. We could not see the trail, and we could only follow it by keeping in the dust cloud. The night was very calm, but occasionally a slight breeze would waft the cloud and disconcert our bearings; then we were obliged to halt to catch a sound from those in advance, sometimes whistling or hallooing, and getting a response we would start forward again. Finally troopers were put ahead, away from the noise of our column, and where they could hear the noise of those in front. A little after 2 a.m., June 25, the command was halted to await further tidings from the scouts; we had marched about ten miles. Part of the command unsaddled to rest the horses. After daylight some coffee was made, but it was almost impossible to drink it; the water was so alkaline that the horses refused to drink it. Some time before eight o'clock, General Custer rode bareback to the several troops and gave orders to be ready to march at eight o'clock, and gave information that scouts had discovered the locality of the Indian villages or camps in the valley of the Little Big Horn, about twelve or fifteen miles beyond the divide. Just before setting out on the march I went to where General Custer's bivouac was. The General, "Bloody Knife," and several Ree scouts and a half-breed interpreter were squatted in a circle having a "talk," after the Indian fashion. The General wore a serious expression and was apparently abstracted. The scouts were doing the talking, and seemed nervous and disturbed. Finally "Bloody Knife" made a remark that recalled the General from his reverie, and he asked in his usual quick, brusque manner, "What's that he says?" The interpreter replied, "He says we'll find enough Sioux to keep us fighting two or three days." The General smiled and remarked, "I guess we'll get through with them in one day."

We started promptly at eight o'clock and marched uninterruptedly until 10:30 a.m., when we halted in a ravine and were ordered to preserve quiet, keep concealed, and not do anything that would be likely to reveal our presence to the enemy; we had marched about ten miles.

It is a rare occurrence in Indian warfare that gives the commander the opportunity to reconnoiter the enemy's position in daylight. This is particularly true if the Indians have a knowledge of the presence of troops in the country. When following an Indian trail the "signs" indicate the length of time elapsed since the presence of the Indians. When the "signs" indicate a "hot trail," *i. e.,* near approach, the commander judges his distance and by a forced march, usually in the night-time, tries to reach the Indian village at night and make his disposition for a surprise attack at daylight. At all events his attack must be made with celerity, and generally without other knowledge of the numbers of the opposing force than that discovered or conjectured while following the trail. The dispositions for the attack may be said to be "made in the dark," and successful surprise to depend upon luck. If the advance to the attack be made in daylight it is next to impossible that a near approach can be made without discovery. In all our previous experiences, when the immediate presence of the troops was known to them, the warriors swarmed to the attack, and resorted to all kinds of ruses to mislead the troops, to delay the advance toward their camp or village, while the squaws and children secured what personal effects they could, drove off the pony herd, and by flight put themselves beyond danger, and then scattering made successful pursuit next to impossible. In civilized warfare the hostile forces may confront each other for hours, days, or weeks, and the battle may be conducted with a tolerable knowledge of the numbers, position, etc., of each other. A full knowledge of the immediate presence of the enemy does not imply immediate attack. In Indian warfare the rule is "touch and go." These remarks are made because the firebrand nature of Indian warfare is not generally understood. In meditating upon the preliminaries of an Indian battle, old soldiers who have participated only in battles of the Rebellion are apt to draw upon their own experiences for comparison, when there is no comparison.

The Little Big Horn River, or the "Greasy Grass" as it is known to the Indians, is a rapid mountain stream, from twenty to forty yards wide, with pebbled bottom, but abrupt, soft banks. The water at the ordinary stage is from two to five feet in depth, depending upon the width of the channel. The general direction of its course is northeasterly down to the Little Big Horn battlefield, where it trends northwesterly to its confluence with the Big Horn River. The other topographical features of the country which concern us in this narrative may be briefly described as follows: Between the Little Big Horn and Big Horn Rivers is a plateau of undulating prairie; between the Little Big Horn and the Rosebud are the Little Chetish or Wolf Mountains. By this it must not be misunderstood as a rocky upheaval chain or spur of mountains, but it is a rough, broken country of considerable elevation, of high precipitous hills and deep narrow gulches. The command had followed the trail up a branch of the Rosebud to within, say, a mile of the summit of these mountains, which form the "divide." Not many miles to our right was the divide between the Little Big Horn and Tulloch's Fork. The creek that drained the watershed to our right and front is now called "Sun-dance," or Benteen's, Creek. The trail, very tortuous, and sometimes dangerous, followed down the bed and valley of this creek, which at that time was dry for the greater part of its length. It was from the divide between the Little Big Horn and the Rosebud that the scouts had discovered the smoke rising above the village, and the pony herds grazing in the valley of the Little Big Horn, somewhere about twelve or fifteen miles away. It was to their point of view that General Custer had gone while the column was halted in the ravine. It was impossible for him to discover more of the enemy than had already been reported by the scouts. In consequence of the high bluffs which screened the village, it was not possible in following the trail to discover more. Nor was there a point of observation near the trail from which further discoveries could be made until the battle was at hand.

It was well known to the Indians that the troops were in the field, and a battle was fully expected by them; but the close proximity of our column was not known to them until the morning of the day of battle. Several young men had left the hostile camp on that morning to go to one of the agencies in Nebraska. They saw the dust made by the column of troops; some of their number returned to the village and gave warning that the troops were coming, so the attack was not a surprise. For two or three days their camp had been pitched on the site where they were attacked. The place was not selected with the view to making that the battle-field of the campaign, but whoever was in the van on their march thought it a good place to camp, put up his tepee, and the others as they arrived followed his example. It is customary among the Indians to camp by bands. The bands usually camp some distance apart, and Indians of the number then together would occupy a territory of several miles along the river valley, and not necessarily within supporting distance of each other. But in view of the possible fulfillment of Sitting Bull's prophecy the village had massed.

Our officers had generally collected in groups and discussed the situation. Some sought solitude and sleep, or meditation. The Ree scouts, who had not been very active for the past day or two, were together and their "medicine man" was anointing them and invoking the Great Spirit to protect them from the Sioux. They

INDIAN HOSTILES WATCHING THE COLUMN'S ADVANCE.

seemed to have become satisfied that we were going to find more
Sioux than we could well take care of. Captain Yates's troop had
lost one of its packs of hard bread during the night march from
our last halting-place on the 24th. He had sent a detail back on
the trail to recover it. Captain Keogh came to where a group of
officers were, and said this detail had returned and reported
that when near the pack they discovered an Indian opening one
of the boxes of hard bread with his tomahawk, and that as soon
as the Indian saw the soldiers he galloped away to the hills out of
range and then moved along leisurely. This information was
taken to the General at once by his brother, Colonel Tom Custer.
The General came back and had "officers' call" sounded. He re-
counted Captain Keogh's report, and also said that the scouts had
seen several Indians moving along the ridge overlooking the valley through which we had marched, as if observing our movements; he thought the Indians must have seen the dust made by
the command. At all events our presence had been discovered and
further concealment was unnecessary; that we would march at

once to attack the village; that he had not intended to make the attack until the next morning, the 26th, but our discovery made it imperative to act at once, as delay would allow the village to scatter and escape. Troop commanders were ordered to make a detail of one non-commissioned officer and six men to accompany the pack; to inspect their troops and report as soon as they were ready to march; that the troops would take their places in the column of march in the order in which reports of readiness were received, and that the last one to report would escort the pack-train.

The inspections were quickly made and the column was soon en route. We crossed the dividing ridge between the Rosebud and Little Big Horn valleys a little before noon. Shortly afterward the regiment was divided into battalions. The advance battalion, under Major Reno, consisted of troop "M," Captain French; troop "A," Captain Moylan and Lieutenant De Rudio; troop "G," Lieutenants McIntosh and Wallace; the Indian scouts under Lieutenants Varnum and Hare and the interpreter Girard; Lieutenant Hodgson was Acting Adjutant and Doctors De Wolf and Porter were the medical officers. The battalion under General Custer was composed of troop "I," Captain Keogh and Lieutenant Porter; troop "F," Captain Yates and Lieutenant Reily; troop "C," Captain Custer and Lieutenant Harrington; troop "E," Lieutenants Smith and Sturgis; troop "L," Lieutenants Calhoun and Crittenden; Lieutenant Cook was the Adjutant, and Dr. G. E. Lord was medical officer. The battalion under Captain Benteen consisted of troop "H," Captain Benteen and Lieutenant Gibson; troop "D," Captain Weir and Lieutenant Edgerly, and troop "K," Lieutenant Godfrey. The pack-train, Lieutenant Mathey in charge, was under the escort of troop "B," Captain McDougall.

Major Reno's battalion marched down a valley that developed into the small tributary to the Little Big Horn, now called "Sun-dance," or Benteen's, Creek. The Indian trail followed the meanderings of this valley. Custer's column followed Reno's closely, and the pack-train followed their trail. Benteen's battalion was ordered to the left and front, to a line of high bluffs about three or four miles distant. Benteen was ordered if he saw anything to send word to Custer, but to pitch into anything he came across; if, when he arrived at the high bluffs, he could not see any enemy, he should continue his march to the next line of bluffs and so on, until he could see the Little Big Horn Valley. He marched over a succession of rough, steep hills and deep valleys. The view from the point where the regiment was organized into battalions did not discover the difficult nature of the country, but as we advanced farther it became more and more difficult and more forbidding. Lieutenant Gibson was sent some distance in advance but saw no enemy, and so signaled the result of his reconnaissance to Benteen. The obstacles threw the battalion by degrees to the right until we came in sight of and not more than a mile from the trail. Many of our horses were greatly jaded by the climbing and descending, some getting far to the rear of the column. Benteen very wisely determined to follow the trail of the rest of the command, and we got into it just in advance of the pack-train. During this march on the left we could see occasionally the battalion under Custer, distinguished by the troop mounted on gray horses, marching at a rapid gait. Two or three times we heard loud cheering and also some few shots, but the occasion of these demonstrations is not known.

CAPTAIN KEOGH

Some time after getting on the trail we came to a water-hole, or morass, at which a stream of running water had its source. Benteen halted the battalion. While watering we heard some firing in advance, and Weir became a little impatient at the delay of watering and started off with his troop, taking the advance, whereas his place in column was second. The rest of the battalion moved out very soon afterward and soon caught up with him. Just as we were leaving the water-hole the pack-train was arriving, and the poor thirsty mules plunged into the morass in spite of the efforts of the packers to prevent them, for they had not had water since the previous evening. We passed a burning tepee, fired presumably by our scouts, in which was the body of a warrior who had been killed in the battle with Crook's troops on the Rosebud on the 17th of June.

The battalions under Reno and Custer did not meet any Indians until Reno arrived at the burning tepee; here a few were seen. These Indians did not act as if surprised by the appearance of troops; they made no effort to delay the column, but simply kept far enough in advance to invite pursuit. Reno's command and the scouts followed them closely, until he received orders "to move forward at as rapid a gait as he thought prudent, and charge the village afterward, and the whole outfit would support him." The order was received when Reno was not very far from the Little Big Horn River. His battalion moved at a trot to the river, where Reno delayed about ten or fifteen minutes watering the horses and reforming the column on the left bank of the stream. Reno now sent word to Custer that he had everything in front of him and that the enemy was strong. Custer had moved off to the right, being separated from Reno by a line of high bluffs and the river. Reno moved forward in column of fours about half a mile, then formed the battalion in line of battle across the valley with the scouts on the left; after advancing about a mile further he deployed the battalion as skirmishers. In the mean time the Hostiles, continually reinforced, fell back, firing occasionally, but made no decided effort to check Reno's advance. The horses of two men became unmanageable and carried them into the Indian camp. The Indians now developed great force, opened a brisk fire, mounted, and made a dash toward the foot-hills on the left flank where the Ree scouts were. The scouts ignominiously fled, most of them abandoning the field altogether.

Reno, not seeing the "whole outfit" within supporting distance, did not obey his orders to charge the village, but dismounted his command to fight on foot. The movements of the Indians around the left flank and the flight of the scouts caused the left to fall back until the command was on the defensive in the timber and covered by the bank of the old river-bed. Reno's loss thus far was one wounded. The position was a strong one, well protected in front by the bank and fringe of timber, somewhat open in the rear, but sheltered by timber in the bottom. Those present differ in their estimates of the length of time the command remained in the bottom after they were attacked in force. Some say "a few minutes"; others, "about an hour." While Reno remained there his casualties were few. The Hostiles had him nearly surrounded, and there was some firing from the rear of the position by Indians on the opposite bank of the river. One man was killed close to

UNHORSED.

where Reno was, and directly afterward Reno gave orders to those near him to "mount and get to the bluffs." This order was not generally heard or communicated; while those who did hear it were preparing to execute it, he countermanded the order, but soon afterward he repeated the same order, "to mount and get to the bluffs," and again it was not generally understood. Individuals, observing the preparations of those on the left, near Reno, informed their troop commanders, who then gave orders to mount. Owing to the noise of the firing and to the absorbed attention they were giving to the enemy, many did not know of the order until too late to accompany the command. Some remained concealed until the Indians left and then came out. Four others remained until night and then escaped. Reno's command left the bottom by troop organizations in column. Reno was with the foremost in this retreat or "charge," as he termed it in his report, and after he

RIVER CROSSING WHERE RENO WITHDREW FROM THE VALLEY.

had exhausted the shots of his revolvers he threw them away. The hostile strength pushed Reno's retreat to the left, so he could not get to the ford where he had entered the valley, but they were fortunate in striking the river at a fordable place; a pony-trail led up a funnel-shaped ravine into the bluffs. Here the command got jammed and lost all semblance of organization. The Indians fired into them, but not very effectively. There does not appear to have been any resistance, certainly no organized resistance, during this retreat. On the right and left of the ravine into which the pony-path led were rough precipitous clay bluffs. It was surprising to see what steep inclines men and horses clambered up under the excitement of danger.

Lieutenant Donald McIntosh was killed soon after leaving the timber. Dr. De Wolf was killed while climbing one of the bluffs a short distance from the command. Lieutenant B. H. Hodgson's

THE RIVER AND (RIGHT) THE BLUFF TO WHICH RENO RETIRED.

horse leaped from the bank into the river and fell dead; the lieutenant was wounded in the leg, probably by the same bullet that killed the horse. Hodgson called out, "For God's sake, don't abandon me"; he was assured that he would not be left behind. Hodgson then took hold of a comrade's stirrup-strap and was taken across the stream, but soon after was shot and killed. Hodgson, some days before the battle, had said that if he was dismounted in battle or wounded, he intended to take hold of somebody's stirrup to assist himself from the field. During the retreat Private Dalvern, troop "F," had a hand-to-hand conflict with an Indian; his horse was killed; he then shot the Indian, caught the Indian's pony, and rode to the command.

Reno's casualties thus far were three officers, including Dr. J. M. De Wolf, and twenty-nine enlisted men and scouts killed; seven enlisted men wounded; and one officer, one interpreter, and fourteen soldiers and scouts missing. Nearly all the casualties occurred during the retreat and after leaving the timber. The Ree scouts continued their flight until they reached the supply camp at the mouth of the Powder, on the 27th. The Crow scouts remained with the command.

We will now go back to Benteen's battalion. Not long after leaving the water-hole a sergeant met him with an order from Custer to the commanding officer of the pack-train to hurry it up. The sergeant was sent back to the train with the message; as he passed the column he said to the men, "We've got 'em, boys." From this and other remarks we inferred that Custer had attacked and captured the village.

Shortly afterward we were met by a trumpeter bearing this message signed by Colonel Cook, Adjutant: "Benteen, come on. Big village. Be quick. Bring packs," with the postscript, "Bring packs." The column had been marching at a trot and walk, according as the ground was smooth or broken. We now heard firing, first straggling shots, and as we advanced the engagement became more and more pronounced and appeared to be coming toward us. The column took the gallop with pistols drawn, expecting to meet the enemy which we thought Custer was driving before him in his effort to communicate with the pack-train, never suspecting that our force had been defeated. We were forming in line to meet our supposed enemy, when we came in full view of the valley of the Little Big Horn. The valley was full of horsemen riding to and fro in clouds of dust and smoke, for the grass had been fired by the Indians to drive the troops out and cover their own movements. On the bluffs to our right we saw a body of troops and that they were engaged. But an engagement appeared to be going on in the valley too. Owing to the distance, smoke, and dust, it was impossible to distinguish if those in the valley were friends or foes. There was a short time of uncertainty as to the direction in which we should go, but some Crow scouts came by, driving a small herd of ponies, one of whom said "Soldiers," and motioned for the command to go to the right. Following his directions, we soon joined Reno's battalion, which was still firing. Reno had lost his hat and had a handkerchief tied about his head, and appeared to be very much excited.

Lt. Hodgson

Benteen's battalion was ordered to dismount and deploy as skirmishers on the edge of the bluffs overlooking the valley. Very soon after this the Indians withdrew from the attack. Lieutenant Hare came to where I was standing and, grasping my hand heartily, said with a good deal of emphasis: "We've had a big fight in the bottom, got whipped, and I am —— glad to see you." I was satisfied that he meant what he said, for I had already suspected that something was wrong, but was not quite prepared for such startling information. Benteen's battalion was ordered to divide its ammunition with Reno's men, who had apparently expended nearly all in their personal possession. It has often been a matter of doubt whether this was a fact, or the effect of imagination. It seems most improbable, in view of their active movements and the short time the command was firing, that the "most of the men" should have expended one hundred and fifty rounds of ammunition per man.

While waiting for the ammunition pack-mules, Major Reno concluded to make an effort to recover and bury the body of Lieutenant Hodgson. At the same time we loaded up a few men with canteens to get water for the command; they were to accompany the rescuing party. The effort was futile; the party was ordered back after being fired upon by some Indians who doubtless were scalping the dead near the foot of the bluffs.

A number of officers collected on the edge of the bluff overlooking the valley and were discussing the situation; among our number was Captain Moylan, a veteran soldier, and a good one too, watching intently the scene below. Moylan remarked, quite emphatically: "Gentlemen, in my opinion General Custer has made the biggest mistake of his life, by not taking the whole regiment in at once in the first attack." At this time there were a large number of horsemen, Indians, in the valley. Suddenly they all started down the valley, and in a few minutes scarcely a horseman was to be seen. Heavy firing was heard down the river. During this time the questions were being asked: "What's the matter with Custer, that he don't send word what we shall do?" "Wonder what we are staying here for?" etc., thus showing some uneasiness; but still no one seemed to show great anxiety, nor do I know that any one felt any serious apprehension but that Custer could and would take care of himself. Some of Reno's men had seen a party of Custer's command, including Custer himself, on the bluffs about the time the Indians began to develop in Reno's front. This party was heard to cheer, and seen to wave their hats as if to give encouragement, and then they disappeared behind the hills or escaped further attention from those below. It was about the time of this incident that Trumpeter Martini left Cook with Custer's last orders to Benteen, viz.: "Benteen, come on. Big village. Be quick. Bring packs. Cook, Adjutant. P.S. Brink packs." The repetition in the order would seem to indicate that Cook was excited, flurried, or that he wanted to emphasize the necessity for escorting the packs. It is possible, yes probable, that from the high point Custer could then see nearly the whole camp and force of the Indians and realized that the chances were desperate; but it was too late to reunite his forces for the attack. Reno was already in the fight and his (Custer's) own battalion was separated from the attack by a distance of two and a half to three miles. He had no reason to think that Reno would not push his attack vigorously. A commander seldom goes into battle counting upon the failure of his lieutenant; if he did, he certainly would provide that such failure should not turn into disaster.

LT. COOK

During a long time after the junction of Reno and Benteen we heard firing down the river in the direction of Custer's command. We were satisfied that Custer was fighting the Indians somewhere, and the conviction was expressed that "our command ought to be doing something or Custer would be after Reno with a sharp stick." We heard two distinct volleys which excited some surprise, and, if I mistake not, brought out the remark from some one that "Custer was giving it to them for all he was worth." I have but little doubt now that these volleys were fired by Custer's orders as signals of distress and to indicate where he was.

Captain Weir and Lieutenant Edgerly, after driving the Indians away from Reno's command, on their side, heard the firing, became impatient at the delay, and thought they would move down that way, if they should be permitted. Weir started to get this permission, but changed his mind and concluded to take a survey from the high bluffs first. Edgerly, seeing Weir going in the direction of the firing, supposed it was all right and started down the ravine with the troop. Weir, from the high point, saw the Indians in large numbers start for Edgerly, and signaled for him to change his direction, and Edgerly went over to the high point, where they remained, not seriously molested, until the remainder of the troops marched down there; the Indians were seen by them to ride about what afterward proved to be Custer's battle-field, shooting into the bodies of the dead men.

McDougall came up with the pack-train and reported the firing when he reported his arrival to Reno. I remember distinctly looking at my watch at twenty minutes past four, and made a note of it in my memorandum-book, and although I have never satisfactorily been able to recall what particular incident happened at that time, it was some important event before we started down the river. It is my impression, however, that it was the arrival of the pack-train. It was about this time that thirteen men and a scout named Herendeen rejoined the command; they had been missing since Reno's flight from the bottom; several of them were wounded. These men had lost their horses in the stampede from the bottom and had remained in the timber; when leaving the timber to rejoin, they were fired upon by five Indians, but they drove them away and were not again molested.

My recollection is that it was about half-past two when we joined Reno. About five o'clock the command moved down toward Custer's supposed whereabouts, intending to join him. The advance went as far as the high bluffs where the command was halted. Persons who have been on the plains and have seen stationary objects dancing before them, now in view and now obscured, or a weed on the top of a hill, projected against the sky, magnified to appear as a tree, will readily understand why our views would be unsatisfactory. We could see stationary groups of horsemen, and individual horsemen moving about; from their grouping and the manner in which they sat their horses we knew they were Indians. On the left of the valley a strange sight attracted our attention. Some one remarked that there had been a fire that scorched the leaves of the bushes, which caused the reddish-brown appearance, but this appearance was changeable; watching this intently for a short time with field-glasses, it was discovered that this strange sight was the immense pony-herds of the Indians.

Looking toward Custer's field, on a hill two miles away we saw a large assemblage. At first our command did not appear to attract their attention, although there was some commotion observable among those nearer to our position. We heard occasional shots, most of which seemed to be a great distance off, beyond the large groups on the hill. While watching this group the conclusion was arrived at that Custer had been repulsed, and the firing was the parting shots of the rear-guard. The firing ceased, the groups dispersed, clouds of dust arose from all parts of the field, and the horsemen converged toward our position. The command was now dismounted to fight on foot. Weir's and French's troops were posted on the high bluffs and to the front of them; my own troop along the crest of the bluffs next to the river; the rest of the command moved to the rear, as I supposed to occupy other points in the vicinity, to make this our defensive position. Busying myself with posting my men, giving direction about the use of ammunition, etc., I was a little startled by the remark that the command was out of sight. At this time Weir's and French's troops were being attacked. Orders were soon brought to me by Lieutenant Hare, Acting-Adjutant, to join the main command. I had gone some distance in the execution of this order when, looking back, I saw French's troop come tearing over the bluffs, and soon after Weir's troop followed in hot haste. Edgerly was near the top of the bluff trying to mount his frantic horse, and it did seem that

MOVING THE LED HORSES AWAY FROM THE FIRI

he would not succeed, but he vaulted into his saddle and then
joined the troop. The Indians almost immediately followed to

NE WHILE THE TROOPERS FIGHT DISMOUNTED.

the top of the bluff, and commenced firing into the retreating
troops, killing one man, wounding others and several horses.

They then started down the hillside in pursuit. I at once made up my mind that such a retreat and close pursuit would throw the whole command into confusion, and, perhaps, prove disastrous. I dismounted my men to fight on foot, deploying as rapidly as possible without waiting for the formation laid down in tactics. Lieutenant Hare expressed his intention of staying with me, "Adjutant or no Adjutant." The led horses were sent to the main command. Our fire in a short time compelled the Indians to halt and take cover, but before this was accomplished, a second order came for me to fall back as quickly as possible to the main command. Having checked the pursuit we began our retreat, slowly at first, but kept up our firing. After proceeding some distance the men began to group together, and to move a little faster and faster, and our fire slackened. This was pretty good evidence that they were getting demoralized. The Indians were being heavily reinforced, and began to come from their cover, but kept up a heavy fire. I halted the line, made the men take their intervals, and again drove the Indians to cover; then once more began the retreat. The firing of the Indians was very heavy; the bullets struck the ground all about us; but the "ping-ping" of the bullets overhead seemed to have a more terrifying influence than the "swish-thud" of the bullets that struck the ground immediately about us. When we got to the ridge in front of Reno's position I observed some Indians making all haste to get possession of a hill to the right. I could now see the rest of the command, and I knew that that hill would command Reno's position. Supposing that my troop was to occupy the line we were then on, I ordered Hare to take ten men and hold the hill, but, just as he was moving off, an order came from Reno to get back as quickly as possible; so I recalled Hare and ordered the men to run to the lines. This movement was executed, strange to say, without a single casualty.

The Indians now took possession of all the surrounding high

points, and opened a heavy fire. They had in the mean time sent a large force up the valley, and soon our position was entirely surrounded. It was now about seven o'clock.

Our position next the river was protected by the rough, rugged steep bluffs which were cut up by irregular deep ravines. From the crest of these bluffs the ground gently declined away from the river. On the north there was a short ridge, the ground sloping gently to the front and rear. This ridge, during the first day, was occupied by five troops. Directly in rear of the ridge was a small hill; in the ravine on the south of this hill our hospital was established, and the horses and pack-mules were secured. Across this ravine one troop, Moylan's, was posted, the packs and dead animals being utilized for breastworks. The high hill on the south was occupied by Benteen's troop. Everybody now lay down and spread himself out as thin as possible. After lying there a few minutes I was horrified to find myself wondering if a small sagebush, about as thick as my finger, would turn a bullet, so I got up and walked along the line, cautioned the men not to waste their ammunition; ordered certain men who were good shots to do the firing, and others to keep them supplied with loaded guns.

The firing continued till nearly dark (between nine and ten o'clock), although after dusk but little attention was paid to the firing, as everybody moved about freely.

Of course everybody was wondering about Custer — why he did not communicate by courier or signal. But the general opinion seemed to prevail that he had been defeated and driven down the river, where he would probably join General Terry, and with whom he would return to our relief. Quite frequently, too, the question, "What's the matter with Custer?" would evoke an impatient reply.

Indians are proverbial economists of fuel, but they did not stint themselves that night. The long twilight was prolonged by numerous bonfires, located throughout their village. The long shadows of the hills and the refracted light gave a supernatural aspect to the surrounding country, which may account for the illusions of those who imagined they could see columns of troops, etc. Although our dusky foes did not molest us with obtrusive attentions during the night, yet it must not be inferred that we were allowed to pass the night in perfect rest; or that they were endeavoring to soothe us into forgetfulness of their proximity, or trying to conceal their situation. They were a good deal happier than we were; nor did they strive to conceal their joy. Their camp was a veritable pandemonium. All night long they continued their frantic revels; beating tom-toms, dancing, whooping, yelling with demoniacal screams, and discharging firearms. We knew they were having a scalp-dance. In this connection the question has often been asked "if they did not have prisoners at the torture?" The Indians deny that they took any prisoners. We did not discover any evidence of torture in their camps. It is true that we did find human heads severed from their bodies, but these probably had been paraded in their orgies during that terrible night.

Our casualties had been comparatively few since taking position on the hill. The question of moving was discussed, but the conditions coupled to the proposition caused it to be indignantly rejected. Some of the scouts were sent out soon after dark to look for signs of Custer's command, but they returned after a short absence saying that the country was full of Sioux. Lieutenant Varnum volunteered to go out, but was either discouraged from the venture or forbidden to go out.

After dark the troops were arranged a little differently. The horses were unsaddled, and the mules were relieved of their packs; all animals were secured to lariats stretched and picketed to the ground.

Soon after all firing had ceased the wildest confusion prevailed.

Men imagined they could see a column of troops over on the hills or ridges, that they could hear the tramp of the horses, the command of officers, or even the trumpet-calls. Stable-call was sounded by one of our trumpeters; shots were fired by some of our men, and familiar trumpet-calls were sounded by our trumpeter immediately after, to let the supposed marching column know that we were friends. Every favorable expression or opinion was received with credulity, and then ratified with a cheer. Somebody suggested that General Crook might be coming, so some one, a civilian packer, I think, mounted a horse, and galloping along the line yelled: "Don't be discouraged, boys, Crook is coming." But they gradually realized that the much-wished-for reinforcements were but the phantasma of their imaginations, and settled down to their work of digging rifle-pits. They worked in pairs, in threes and fours. The ground was hard and dry. There were only three or four spades and shovels in the whole command; axes, hatchets, knives, tableforks, tin cups, and halves of canteens were brought into use. However, everybody worked hard, and some were still digging when the enemy opened fire at early dawn, between half-past two and three o'clock, so that all had some sort of shelter, except Benteen's men. The enemy's first salutations were rather feeble, and our side made scarcely any response; but as dawn advanced to daylight their lines were heavily reinforced, and both sides kept up a continuous fusillade. Of course it was their policy to draw our fire as much as possible to exhaust our ammunition. As they exposed their persons very little we forbade our men, except well-known good shots, to fire without orders. The Indians amused themselves by standing erect, in full view for an instant, and then dropping down again before a bullet could reach them, but of that they soon seemed to grow tired or found it too dangerous; then they resorted to the old ruse of raising a hat and blouse, or a blanket, on a stick to draw our fire; we soon understood their tactics. Occasionally they fired volleys at command. Their fire, however, was not very effective. Benteen's troop suffered greater losses than any other, because their rear was exposed to the long-range firing from the hills on the north. The horses and mules suffered greatly, as they were fully exposed to long-range fire from the east.

Benteen came over to where Reno was lying, and asked for reinforcements to be sent to his line. Before he left his line, however, he ordered Gibson not to fall back under any circumstances, as this was the key of the position. Gibson's men had expended nearly all their ammunition, some men being reduced to as few as four or five cartridges. He was embarrassed, too, with quite a number of wounded men. Indeed, the situation here was most critical, for if the Indians had made a rush, a retreat was inevitable. Private McDermott volunteered to carry a message from Gibson to Benteen urging him to hasten the reinforcements. After considerable urging by Benteen, Reno finally ordered French to take "M" troop over to the south side. On his way over Benteen picked up some men then with the horses. Just previous to his arrival an Indian had shot one of Gibson's men, then rushed up and touched the body with his "coup-stick," and started back to cover, but he was killed. He was in such close proximity to the lines and so exposed to the fire that the other Indians could not carry his body away. This, I believe, was the only dead Indian left in our possession. This boldness determined Benteen to make a charge, and the Indians were driven nearly to the river. On their retreat they dragged several dead and wounded warriors away with them.

The firing almost ceased for a while, and then it recommenced with greater fury. From this fact, and their more active movements, it became evident that they contemplated something more serious than a mere fusillade. Benteen came back to where Reno was, and said if something was not done pretty soon the Indians would run into our lines. Waiting a short time, and no action being taken on his suggestion, he said rather impatiently: "You've got to do something here pretty quick; this won't do, you must drive them back." Reno then directed us to get ready for a charge, and told Benteen to give the word. Benteen called out "All ready now, men. Now's your time. Give them hell. Hip, hip, here we go!" and away we went with a hurrah, every man, but one who lay in his pit crying like a child. The Indians fired more rapidly than before from their whole line. Our men left the pits with their carbines loaded, and they began firing without orders soon after we started. A large body of Indians had assembled at the foot of one of the hills, intending probably to make a charge, as Benteen had divined, but they broke as soon as our line started. When we had advanced 75 or 100 yards, Reno called out "Get back, men, get back," and back the whole line came. A most singular fact of this sortie was that not a man who advanced with the lines was hit; but directly after every one had gotten into the pits again, the one man who did not go out was shot in the head and killed instantly. The poor fellow had a premonition that he would be killed, and had so told one of his comrades.

In this narrative of the movements immediately preceding, and resulting in, the annihilation of the men with Custer, I have related facts substantially as observed by myself or as given to me by Chief Gall of the Sioux. His statements have been corroborated by other Indians, notably the wife of "Spotted Horn Bull," an intelligent Sioux squaw, one of the first who had the courage to talk freely to any one who participated in the battle.

In 1886, on the tenth anniversary, an effort was made to have a reunion of the survivors at the battle-field. Colonel Benteen, Captains McDougall and Edgerly, Dr. Porter, Sergeant Hall, Trumpeter Penwell, and myself met there on the 25th of June.

Through the kind efforts of the officers and of the ladies at Fort Custer our visit was made as pleasant as possible. Through the personal influence of Major McLaughlin, Indian agent at Standing Rock Agency, Chief Gall was prevailed upon to accompany the party and describe Custer's part in the battle. We were unfortunate in not having an efficient and truthful interpreter on the field at the reunion. The statements I have used were, after our return to the agency, interpreted by Mrs. McLaughlin and Mr. Farribault, of the agency, both of whom are perfectly trustworthy and are familiar with the Sioux language.

It has been previously noted that General Custer separated from Reno before the latter crossed the Little Big Horn under orders to charge the village. Custer's column bore to the right of the river (a sudden change of plan, probably); a ridge of high bluffs and the river separated the two commands, and they could not see each other. On this ridge, however, Custer and staff were seen to wave their hats, and heard to cheer just as Reno was beginning the attack; but Custer's troops were at that time a mile or more to his right. It was about this time that the trumpeter was sent back with Custer's last order to Benteen. From this place [see A on map] Custer could survey the valley for several miles above and for a short distance below Reno; yet he could only see a part of the village; he must, then, have felt confident that all the Indians were below him; hence, I presume, his message to Benteen. The view of the main body of the village was cut off by the highest points of the ridge, a short distance from him. Had he gone to this high point he would have understood the magnitude of his undertaking, and it is probable that his plan of battle would have been changed. We have no evidence that he did not go there. He could see, however, that the village was not breaking away toward the Big Horn Mountains. He must, then, have expected to find the squaws and children fleeing to the bluffs on

A VIEW OF CUSTER'S HILL IN THE 1890'S.

the north, for in no other way do I account for his wide detour to the right. He must have counted upon Reno's success, and fully expected the "scatteration" of the non-combatants with the pony herds. The probable attack upon the families and the capture of the herds were in that event counted upon to strike consternation in the hearts of the warriors, and were elements for success upon which General Custer fully counted in the event of a daylight attack.

When Reno's advance was checked, and his left began to fall back, Chief Gall started with some of his warriors to cut off Reno's retreat to the bluffs. On his way he was excitedly hailed by "Iron Cedar," one of his warriors, who was on the high point, to hurry to him, that more soldiers were coming. This was the first intimation the Indians had of Custer's column; up to the time of this incident they had supposed that all the troops were in at Reno's attack. Custer had then crossed the valley of the dry creek, and was marching along and well up the slope of the bluff forming the second ridge back from the river, and nearly parallel to it. The command was marching rapidly in column of fours, and there was some confusion in the ranks, due probably to the unmanageableness of some excited horses.

The accepted theory for many years after the battle, and still persisted in by some writers, was that Custer's column had turned the high bluffs near the river, moved down the dry (Reno's) creek, and attempted to ford the river near the lowest point of these bluffs; that he was there met by an overpowering force and driven back; that he then divided his battalion, moved down the river with the view of attacking the village, but met with such resistance from the enemy posted along the river bank and ravines that he was compelled to fall back, fighting, to the position on the ridge. The numerous bodies found scattered between the river and ridge were supposed to be the first victims of the fight. I am now satisfied that these were men who either survived those on the ridge or attempted to escape the massacre.

Custer's route was as indicated on the map, and his column was never nearer the river or village than his final position on the ridge. The wife of Spotted Horn Bull, when giving me her account of the battle, persisted in saying that Custer's column did not attempt to cross at the ford, and appealed to her husband, who supported her statement. On the battle-field, in 1886, Chief Gall indicated Custer's route to me, and it then flashed upon me that I myself had seen Custer's trail. On June 28, while we were burying the dead, I asked Major Reno's permission to go on the high ridge east or back of the field to look for tracks of shod horses to ascertain if some of the command might not have escaped. When I reached the ridge I saw this trail, and wondered who could have made it, but dismissed the thought that it had been made by Custer's column, because it did not accord with the theory with which we were then filled, that Custer had attempted to cross at the ford, and this trail was too far back, and showed no indication of leading toward the ford. Trumpeter Penwell was my orderly and accompanied me. It was a singular coincidence that in 1886 Penwell was stationed at Fort Custer, and was my orderly when visiting the battle-field. Penwell corroborated my recollection of the trail.

The ford theory arose from the fact that we found there numerous tracks of shod horses, but they evidently had been made after the Indians had possessed themselves of the cavalry horses, for they rode them after capturing them. No bodies of men or horses were found anywhere near the ford, and these facts are conclusive to my mind that Custer did not go to the ford with any body of men.

GALL

As soon as Gall had personally confirmed Iron Cedar's report he sent word to the warriors battling against Reno, and to the people in the village. The greatest consternation prevailed among the families, and orders were given for them to leave at once. Before they could do so the great body of warriors had left Reno, and hastened to attack Custer. This explains why Reno was not pushed when so much confusion at the river crossing gave the Indians every opportunity of annihilating his command. Not long after the Indians began to show a strong force in Custer's front, Custer turned his column to the left, and advanced in the direction of the village to near a place now marked as a spring, halted at the junction of the ravines just below it, and dismounted two troops, Keogh's and Calhoun's, to fight on foot. These two troops advanced at double-time to a knoll, now marked by Crittenden's monument. The other three troops, mounted, followed them a short distance in their rear. The led horses remained where the troops dismounted. When Keogh and Calhoun got to the knoll the other troops marched rapidly to the right; Smith's troop deployed as skirmishers, mounted, and took position on a ridge, which, on Smith's left, ended in Keogh's position (now marked

by Crittenden's monument) , and, on Smith's right, ended at the hill on which Custer took position with Yates and Tom Custer's troops, now known as Custer's Hill, and marked by the monument erected to the command. Smith's skirmishers, holding their gray horses, remained in groups of fours.

The line occupied by Custer's battalion was the first considerable ridge back from the river, the nearest point being about a half mile from it. His front was extended about three fourths of a mile. The whole village was in full view. A few hundred yards from his line was another but lower ridge, the further slope of which was not commanded by his line. It was here that the Indians under Crazy Horse from the lower part of the village, among whom were the Cheyennes, formed for the charge on Custer's Hill. All Indians had now left Reno. Gall collected his warriors, and moved up a ravine south of Keogh and Calhoun. As they were turning this flank they discovered the led horses without any other guard than the horse-holders. They opened fire upon the horse-holders, and used the usual devices to stampede the horses — that is, yelling, waving blankets, etc.; in this they succeeded very soon, and the horses were caught up by the squaws. In this disaster Keogh and Calhoun probably lost their reserve ammunition, which was carried in the saddle-bags. Gall's warriors now moved to the foot of the knoll held by Calhoun. A large force dismounted and advanced up the slope far enough to be able to see the soldiers when standing erect, but were protected when squatting or lying down. By jumping up and firing quickly, they exposed themselves only for an instant, but drew the fire of the soldiers, causing a waste of ammunition. In the mean time Gall was massing his mounted warriors under the protection of the slope. When everything was in readiness, at a signal from Gall the dismounted warriors rose, fired, and every Indian gave voice to the war-whoop; the mounted Indians put whip to their ponies, and the whole mass rushed upon and crushed Calhoun. The maddened mass of Indians was carried forward by its own momentum over Calhoun and Crittenden down into the depression where Keogh was, with over thirty men, and all was over on that part of the field.

In the mean time the same tactics were being pursued and executed around Custer's Hill. The warriors, under the leadership of Crow-King, Crazy Horse, White Bull, "Hump," and others, moved up the ravine west of Custer's Hill, and concentrated under the shelter of the ridges on his right flank and back of his position. Gall's bloody work was finished before the annihilation of Custer was accomplished, and his victorious warriors hurried forward to the hot encounter then going on, and the frightful massacre was completed.

Smith's men had disappeared from the ridge, but not without leaving enough dead bodies to mark their line. About twenty-eight bodies of men belonging to this troop and other organizations were found in one ravine nearer the river. Many corpses were found scattered over the field between Custer's line of defense, the river, and in the direction of Reno's hill. These, doubtless, were of men who had attempted to escape; some of them may have been sent as couriers by Custer. One of the first bodies I recognized and one of the nearest to the ford was that of Sergeant Butler of Tom Custer's troop. Sergeant Butler was a soldier of many years' experience and of known courage. The indications were that he had sold his life dearly, for near and under him were found many empty cartridge-shells.

All the Indian accounts that I know of agree that there was no organized close-quarter fighting, except on the two flanks; that with the annihilation at Custer's Hill the battle was virtually over. It does not appear that the Indians made any advance to the attack from the direction of the river; they did have a defensive

Lt. Sturgis

Lt. Harrington

force along the river and in the ravines which destroyed those who left Custer's line.

There was a great deal of firing going on over the field after the battle by the young men and boys riding about and shooting into the dead bodies.

Tuesday morning, June 27, we had reveille without the "morning guns," enjoyed the pleasure of a square meal, and had our stock properly cared for. Our commanding officer seemed to think the Indians had some "trap" set for us, and required our men to hold themselves in readiness to occupy the pits at a moment's notice. Nothing seemed determined except to stay where we were. Not an Indian was in sight, but a few ponies were seen grazing down in the valley.

About 9:30 a.m. a cloud of dust was observed several miles down the river. The assembly was sounded, the horses were placed in a protected situation, and camp-kettles and canteens were filled with water. An hour of suspense followed; but from the slow advance we concluded that they were our own troops. "But whose command is it?" We looked in vain for a gray-horse troop. It could not be Custer; it must then be Crook, for if it was Terry, Custer would be with him. Cheer after cheer was given for Crook. A white man, Harris, I think, soon came up with a note from General Terry, addressed to General Custer, dated June 26, stating that two of our Crow scouts had given information that our column had been whipped and nearly all had been killed; that he did not believe their story, but was coming with medical assistance. The scout said that he could not get to our lines the night before, as the Indians were on the alert. Very soon after this Lieutenant Bradley, 7th Infantry, came into our lines, and asked where I was. Greeting most cordially my old friend, I immediately asked, "Where is Custer?" He replied, "I don't know, but I suppose he was killed, as we counted 197 dead bodies. I don't suppose any escaped." We were simply dumfounded. This was the first intimation we had of his fate. It was hard to realize; it did seem impossible.

General Terry and staff, and officers of General Gibbon's column soon after approached, and their coming was greeted with prolonged, hearty cheers. The grave countenance of the General awed the men to silence. The officers assembled to meet their guests. There was scarcely a dry eye; hardly a word was spoken, but quivering lips and hearty grasping of hands gave token of thankfulness for the relief and grief for the misfortune.

LT. SMITH

During the rest of that day we were busy collecting our effects and destroying surplus property. The wounded were cared for and taken to the camp of our new friends of the Montana column. Among the wounded was saddler "Mike" Madden of my troop, whom I promoted to be sergeant, on the field, for gallantry. Madden was very fond of his grog. His long abstinence had given him a famous thirst. It was necessary to amputate his leg, which was done without administering any anesthetic; but after the amputation the surgeon gave him a good, stiff drink of brandy. Madden eagerly gulped it down, and his eyes fairly danced as he smacked his lips and said, "M-eh, doctor, cut off my other leg."

LT. YATES

On the morning of the 28th we left our intrenchments to bury the dead of Custer's command. The morning was bright, and from the high bluffs we had a clear view of Custer's battle-field. We saw a large number of objects that looked like white boulders scattered over the field. Glasses were brought into requisition, and it was announced that these objects were the dead bodies. Captain Weir exclaimed, "Oh, how white they look!"

All the bodies, except a few, were stripped of their clothing. According to my recollection nearly all were scalped or mutilated, but there was one notable exception, that of General Custer, whose face and expression were natural; he had been shot in the temple and in the left side. Many faces had a pained, almost terrified expression. It is said that "Rain-in-the-face," a Sioux warrior, has gloried that he had cut out and had eaten the heart and liver of one of the officers. Other bodies were mutilated in a disgusting manner. The bodies of Dr. Lord and Lieutenants Porter, Harrington, and Sturgis were not found, at least not recognized. The clothing of Porter and Sturgis was found in the village, and showed that they had been killed. We buried, according to my memoranda, 212 bodies. The killed of the entire command was 265, and of wounded we had 52.

The question has been often asked, "What were the causes of Custer's defeat?" I should say:

First. The overpowering numbers of the enemy and their unexpected cohesion.

Second. Reno's panic rout from the valley.

Third. The defective extraction of the empty cartridge-shells from the carbines.

Of the first, I will say that we had nothing conclusive on which to base calculations of the numbers — and to this day it seems almost incredible that such great numbers of Indians should have left the agencies, to combine against the troops, without information relating thereto having been communicated to the commanders of troops in the field, further than that heretofore mentioned. The second has been mentioned incidentally. The Indians say if Reno's position in the valley had been held, they would have been compelled to divide their strength for the different attacks, which would have caused confusion and apprehension, and prevented the concentration of every able-bodied warrior upon the battalion under Custer; that, at the time of the discovery of Custer's advance to attack, the chiefs gave orders for the village to move, to break up; that, at the time of Reno's retreat, this order was being carried out, but as soon as Reno's

TAPS. (CAVALRY BUGLER IN FULL UNIFORM.)

retreat was assured the order was countermanded, and the squaws were compelled to return with the pony herds; that the order would not have been countermanded had Reno's forces remained fighting in the bottom. Custer's attack did not begin until after Reno had reached the bluffs.

Of the third we can only judge by our own experience. When cartridges were dirty and corroded, the ejectors did not always extract the empty shells from the chambers, and the men were compelled to use knives to get them out. When the shells were clean no great difficulty was experienced. To what extent this was a factor in causing the disaster we have no means of knowing.

A battle was unavoidable. Every man in Terry's and Custer's commands expected a battle; it was for that purpose, to punish the Indians, that the command was sent out, and with that determination Custer made his preparations. Had Custer continued his march southward — that is, left the Indian trail — the Indians would have known of our movement on the 25th, and a battle would have been fought very near the same field on which Crook had been attacked and forced back only a week before; the Indians never would have remained in camp and allowed a concentration of the several columns to attack them. If they had escaped without punishment or battle Custer would undoubtedly have been blamed.

COMMENTS BY GENERAL FRY

CAPTAIN GODFREY'S ARTICLE is a valuable contribution to the authentic history of the campaign which culminated in "Custer's Last Battle," June 25, 1876.

The Sioux war of 1876 originated in a request by the Indian Bureau that certain wild and recalcitrant bands of Indians should be compelled to settle down upon their reservations under control of the Indian agent. Sitting Bull, on the Little Missouri in Dakota, and Crazy Horse, on the Powder River, Wyoming, were practically the leaders of the hostile Indians who roamed over what General Sheridan called "an almost totally unknown region, comprising an area of almost 90,000 square miles." The hostile camps contained eight or ten separate bands, each having a chief of its own.

Authority was exercised by a council of chiefs. No chief was endowed with supreme authority, but Sitting Bull was accepted as the leader of all his bands. From 500 to 800 warriors was the most the military authorities thought the hostiles could muster. Sitting Bull's camp, as Custer found it, contained some 8,000 or 10,000 men, women, and children, and about 2,500 warriors, including boys, who were armed with bows and arrows. The men had good firearms, many of them Winchester rifles, with a large supply of ammunition.

War upon this savage force was authorized by the War Department, and was conducted under the direction of Lieutenant-General Sheridan in Chicago.

The campaign opened in the winter, General Sheridan thinking that was the season in which the Indians could be "caught." He directed General Terry to send a mounted column under

Editor's note: Remarks on General Fry's status appear on page 11.

Custer against Sitting Bull, and General Crook to move against Crazy Horse. Bad weather prevented Custer's movement, but Crook advanced March 1. On March 17 he struck Crazy Horse's band, was partially defeated, and the weather being very severe, returned to his base. The repulse of Crook's column, and the inability of Custer to move, gave the Indians confidence, and warriors by the hundred slipped away from the agencies and joined the Hostiles.

In the spring Sheridan's forces resumed the offensive in three isolated columns. The first column under Crook, consisting of 15 companies of cavalry and 5 companies of infantry (total 1,049), marched northward from Fort Fetterman May 29. The second column under General Terry, consisting of the entire 7th Cavalry, 12 companies (about 600 men), 6 companies of infantry, 3 of them on the supply steamboat (400 men), a battery of Gatling guns manned by infantrymen, and 40 Indian scouts, moved westward from Fort A. Lincoln, on the Missouri, May 17.

It happened that while the expedition was being fitted out, Custer unwittingly incurred the displeasure of President Grant, who directed that Custer should not accompany the column. Through his appeal to the President and the intercession of Terry and Sheridan, Custer was permitted to go in command of his regiment, but Terry was required to accompany and command the column. Terry was one of the best of men and ablest of soldiers, but had no experience in Indian warfare.

A third column under General Gibbon (Colonel of Infantry), consisting of 4 companies of cavalry and 6 companies of infantry (450 men all told), marched eastward in April, and united with Terry on the Yellowstone, June 21. When these columns started they were all some 200 or 300 miles from the central position occupied by the enemy. Gibbon was under Terry's control, but Crook and Terry were independent of each other.

The authorities believed that either one of the three columns could defeat the enemy if it "caught" him; otherwise isolated forces would not have been sent to "operate blindly," without means of mutual support, against an enemy in the interior of an almost totally unknown region. Indeed General Sherman said in his official report of 1876, "Up to the moment of Custer's defeat there was nothing, official or private, to justify an officer to expect that any detachment would encounter more than 500 to 800 warriors." The appearance of 2500 to 3000 in the Custer fight, General Sherman adds, "amounted to a demonstration that the troops were dealing, not only with the Hostiles estimated at from 500 to 800, but with the available part of the Agency Indians, who had gone out to help their friends in a fight."

The utter failure of our campaign was due to underestimating the numbers and prowess of the enemy. The strength he was found to possess proved, as General Sherman said in his report, "that the campaign had been planned on wrong premises." Upon this point Gibbon said, "When these various bands succeeded in finding a leader who possessed tact, courage, and ability to concentrate and keep together so large a force, it was only a question of time when one or the other of the exterior columns would meet with a check from the overwhelming numbers of the interior body."

The first result was that Crook's column encountered the enemy, June 17, and was so badly defeated that it was practically out of the campaign.

In his official report Sheridan claims for Crook a "barren victory," but adds, "Next day he returned to his supply camp on Goose Creek and awaited reinforcements and supplies, considering himself too weak to make any movement until additional troops reached him."

On the 21st of June, Terry, with the column from the east,

about one thousand men, was on the south bank of the Yellowstone, at the mouth of the Rosebud. Gibbon was with Terry, and his column from the west, four hundred and fifty men, was some fifteen miles up the Yellowstone on its north bank, nearly opposite the mouth of the Big Horn. The Rosebud and Big Horn flow from south to north about fifteen miles apart, with a high, broken "divide" or ridge between them.

A scouting party had found indications that the Indians were on the Big Horn or its tributaries, and they were found on the 25th about ninety miles away in the valley of the Little Big Horn, with some 2500 warriors. At that time Terry did not imagine them to be so strong, nor did he know that Crook had been defeated on the 17th. He heard nothing of Crook until July 4.

On the night of June 21, Terry held a conference with Gibbon and Custer, at which he says in his annual report in 1876, he decided upon a plan of operations, by which Gibbon was to move south up the Big Horn valley, Custer was to proceed up the Rosebud and ascertain the direction of the Indian trail, and

> if it led to the Little Big Horn it should not be followed, but that Custer should keep still further to the south before turning to the river, in order to intercept the Indians should they attempt to pass around his left, and in order, by a longer march, to give time for Gibbon's column to come up . . . This plan was founded on the belief that the two columns might be brought into coöperating distance of each other, so either of them which should be first engaged might, by a "waiting fight," give time for the other to come up.

Custer's disaster has been directly or by implication attributed to a departure from the "plan." No record of the conference appears to have been made at the time, but Terry's statement concerning it is supported by Gibbon, and no one would dispute it if it stood alone. But it is highly probable that the plan when

Custer moved had neither the force nor importance which it subsequently acquired in Terry's mind. Terry made to Sheridan a full and explicit report, June 27, when the subject was fresh, in which he spoke of the conference, but did not say or intimate that a plan of operations had been decided upon in it. He did say, however, "I informed General Custer I would take the supply steamer up the Yellowstone to ferry General Gibbon's column over the river, that I should personally accompany that column, and that it would in all probability reach the mouth of the Big Horn on the 26th instant." If at that time Terry thought the plan of operations mandatory, he probably would have mentioned it in this report of June 27. It was, however, not until July 2 that he reported the existence of a plan. Then he said in his report to Sheridan made in his own defense, *"I think I owe it to myself* to put you more fully in possession of the facts of the late operations," and followed with the account of the plan, above quoted from his annual report, but did not say that he had issued any orders which Custer had disobeyed.

The plan decided upon in conference on the night of June 21 fixes no blame on Custer. His written instructions from Terry were made June 22, the day after the conference, and they were binding upon him. They made no reference to a plan, but said:

> The Brigadier-General Commanding directs that, as soon as your regiment can be made ready for the march, you will proceed up the Rosebud in pursuit of the Indians whose trail was discovered by Major Reno a few days since. *It is, of course, impossible to give you any definite instructions in regard to this movement,* and were it not impossible to do so the department commander places too much confidence in your zeal, energy and ability to wish to impose upon you precise orders which might hamper your action when nearly in contact with the enemy. He will, however, indicate to you his own views of what your action should be, and he desires

that you should conform to them unless you shall see sufficient reason for departing from them.

The order Custer received was to proceed up the Rosebud in
pursuit of the Indians. Surely he did not disobey that. Everything else was left to his discretion. As Terry did not wish to
hamper Custer's action when nearly in contact with the enemy,
and found it impossible to give precise orders, plainly Custer did
not, could not, disobey orders in any blamable sense, and plainly,
also, he was expected to come "in contact with the enemy."

Captain Godfrey says that the scouts were sent out on the right
flank during the 23d and 24th, moving along the divide between
Rosebud and Tulloch's Fork, from which the valley of the Fork
was in view. It is true Custer does not appear to have examined
the upper part of Tulloch's Creek, but there were no Indians
there, and the omission if it occurred is colorless. He was directed
to endeavor to send a scout through to General Gibbon's column
with the result of his examination of Tulloch's Creek, and was
informed that Gibbon would examine the lower part of the
creek. Whether he endeavored to send a messenger cannot be
ascertained (Captain Godfrey says that a scout named Herendeen
had been selected for this service, and he is of the opinion that
General Custer would have sent him during the day if the fight
had been delayed until early next morning as he at first intended); but nothing concerning Tulloch's Creek was material in
the campaign.

Even conformity to Terry's "views" was expressly left to Custer's discretion.

In his sermon at General Terry's funeral, December 29, 1890,
the Rev. Dr. T. T. Munger said:

Custer's fatal movement was in direct violation of both
verbal and written orders. When his rashness and disobedience ended in the total destruction of his command, General

Terry withheld the fact of the disobeyed orders and suffered an imputation hurtful to his military reputation to rest upon himself, rather than subject a brave but indiscreet subordinate to a charge of disobedience.

When called to account for the accusation which he made against one dead soldier at the Christian burial of another, Dr. Munger gave Colonel R. P. Hughes of the army, a brother-in-law of General Terry and for a long time his aide-de-camp, as authority for his defamatory assertion.

Colonel Hughes denies having authorized Dr. Munger to make the statement, though he admits he was the source of Dr. Munger's information. Called upon more than once, he fails to produce or specify any orders disobeyed by Custer. Indeed there can be no such orders. It is not credible that Terry issued orders which have never been produced by him or any one else, and that these phantom orders if obeyed would have prevented the Custer massacre. Terry was a strict and careful soldier. It was his duty to file with higher authority all the orders he issued in the case, and his orders have passed in due course to their places in public records, and have been discussed above. Custer disobeyed none of them.

Returning to the conference plan of operations, it must be noted that, like the general plan of campaign, it was based upon a misconception of the enemy's strength. It required that a well-armed, wary, and vigilant enemy of unknown strength, some ninety miles away in a country well known to him but unknown to us, should be approached by two columns, the enemy, as it turned out, exceeding in numbers the two columns combined. Even if Custer had gone quite to the south and had not attacked, the plan put it in the power of the enemy to defeat at least one of the columns as he had defeated Crook. Custer no doubt thought if he was strong enough to go to the south and wait to be attacked, he was strong enough to make the attack, and Terry's instructions left the matter to his judgment.

Terry stated in his report that he believed his plan might have resulted in a "waiting fight" through which the column first engaging the enemy might hold him until the other came up, the implication being that advantage from a "waiting fight" was lost through Custer's action. The truth is that a "waiting fight" is exactly what was secured, but there was no advantage in it. Custer's command, south of the enemy, kept him engaged from the 25th until the evening of the 26th, when the column from the north approached. Then the Indians quietly slipped away without the northern column being able to detain or injure them.

Godfrey gives the details of Custer's three days' march and of the fight on the 25th and 26th. When the command was nearly in contact with the enemy Custer directed one company to guard the pack-train, sent three companies under Benteen to the south, no doubt in deference to Terry's advice to see that the Indians did not pass that way, ordered Reno with three companies to charge northward down the valley upon the enemy's flank, and with the rest of his force, some 250 men, galloped down the river about three miles to attack in front. The result is known. It is not bad tactics to throw a part of the attacking force upon the exposed flank of the enemy, and support it by a front attack with the other part, and that is what Custer did. To "support" the flanking force is not necessarily to follow it. Custer's "pursuit" to the field where he "caught" the Indians was rapid, but his defeat is not to be attributed to fatigue of horses or men. The offensive is often more fatiguing than the defensive, but the loss of a battle is seldom, if ever, due to the fatigue of the attacking force.

During the Indian outbreak at Pine Ridge Agency, 1890, a battalion of the 9th Cavalry, under Colonel Henry, accompanied by a section of Light Battery E, 1st Artillery, marched as follows: December 24, between 2:30 p.m. and 3:30 next morning, fifty

CAVALRY OFFICER IN CAMPAIGN DRESS.

miles and six miles further after daylight; scouted actively on the 25th, 26th, and 27th, made forty-four miles on the 28th, and starting at 9:30 a.m. on the 29th made ninety-six miles before 4 p.m. on the 30th; was all the time ready for battle, had a skirmish, and marched six miles after the skirmish, making 102 miles in 30 hours.*

The part taken by the companies under Reno proved that Custer's force was not too tired to go into the fight and maintain it until the evening of the 26th. The command was probably no more fatigued than cavalry usually is when it attacks in a vigorous pursuit.

Having marched leisurely from Fort Lincoln on the Missouri to the Rosebud on the Yellowstone, the men and horses were well seasoned but not worn, and Reno has stated that when the regiment moved out on the 22d of June "the men and officers were cheerful," the *"horses were in best condition."* After Custer "caught" the Indians, their "escape," against which he was warned in Terry's written instructions, could be prevented only by attack. The trouble was their strength was underestimated. Terry reported July 2: "He [Custer] expressed the utmost confidence he had all the force he could need, *and I shared his confidence."* Believing, as he and Sheridan and Terry did, that he was strong enough for victory, if Custer had not attacked, and the Indians had moved away, as they did when Gibbon's column approached on the 26th, Custer would have been condemned, perhaps disgraced. With his six hundred troopers he could not *herd* the Indians, nor, in that vast, wild, and difficult region, with which they were familiar and of which we were ignorant, could he by going further to his left, "south," drive them against Gibbon's column. His fight was forced by the situation. Believing, as

---

*Lieutenant A. W. Perry, in the Journal of U. S. Cavalry Association.

Custer and his superiors did, that his 600 troopers were opposed by only 500, or at most 800 warriors, his attack shows neither desperation nor rashness. General Sherman said that when Custer found himself in presence of the Indians he could do nothing but attack.*

LT. J. CRITTENDEN

In relation to Reno's part, it is proper to state that General Sherman, in his official report, 1876, commends "the brave and prudent conduct of Major Reno," and in 1879 a Court of Inquiry was convened at Reno's request to examine into his conduct in the battle. The court was created by the President and he approved its findings. It reported the facts as it found them, and said "the conduct of the officers throughout was excellent, and while subordinates in some instances did more for the safety of the command by brilliant displays of courage than did Major Reno, there was nothing in his conduct which requires animadversion from this court." Conceding to Reno the right to the benefit of these indorsements, there are some facts which should be noted.

"About the same time that Reno's command was crossing the river in retreat" after it had been engaged only "half an hour or forty-five minutes in all," says the Reno Court of Inquiry, Benteen approached.

His three companies doubled Reno's force, giving him six com-

---

*New York City, May 11, 1891. Dear Fry: In reply to your note I cannot recall the whole conversation between General Sherman and myself. I remember distinctly that I was much distressed and greatly excited. The conversation took place not long after Custer's defeat. I condemned everything and everybody, and doubt not I spoke only words of passion without judgment. I think I said that Custer's command was in no condition to fight when he made the attack. To this, or something like it, Sherman said when Custer found himself in the presence of the Indians, he could do nothing but attack.

Very truly, etc., T. L. Crittenden.

(Editor's Note: General T. L. Crittenden, U. S. A., was the father of Lt. J. Crittenden who fell with Custer.)

panies, whereas Custer had only five. Another company with the pack-train arrived a little later. Custer's need of men and ammunition was shown by his last order which Benteen received before joining Reno. "Come on. Big village. Be quick. Bring pack." Under the circumstances Reno might well have treated this order as applying to him as well as to Benteen. As soon as the Indians had driven him back they concentrated upon Custer.

"During a long time" after Benteen joined Reno, says Godfrey, Custer's firing was heard, showing that his five companies were hotly engaged with the opposing force, which Reno had found too strong. If Reno had marched then with his six companies to the sound of Custer's carbines, it would have been conduct to commend, and might have enabled Custer to extricate the command. When he did move out it was too late; Custer's men had been killed, and the enemy was able to oppose Reno with his whole force and drive him back and invest him in his place of refuge.

Crook's and Terry's columns having been defeated, they were heavily reinforced; and on the 30th of July a staff officer from Chicago arrived at Terry's camp with orders for Terry and Crook to unite. After their junction—August 10—there was much marching, but no fighting. The enemy could not be "caught."

OF THE ILLUSTRATIONS

THE ILLUSTRATIONS in this book were, in the main, reproduced from the pages of the January, 1892 issue of *The Century Magazine* in which Godfrey's narrative first appeared.

In addition, portraits of Godfrey, Terry, Gibbon, Reno and Benteen were borrowed from the extensive collection of Custer materials owned by Mr. Michael Harrison of Sacramento, California. The publisher's special gratitude is expressed for Mr. Harrison's permission to use these as well as for his kindness in providing editorial guidance.

The names of the artists and engravers, where known, are as follows: Page 9, Custer engraved by J. H. E. Whitney after a photograph by Brady; page 14, Godfrey photograph by David F. Barry (original in Denver Public Library); pages 22-3, Troopers and Their Mounts, by Frederic Remington, engraved by "C.A.P."; page 43, Indians Watching by Remington, engraved by "H.O."; page 47, Unhorsed by Remington; pages 48 and 49, Reno's Crossing and Reno's Bluff photographs by Barry; pages 56-57, Moving Led Horses by Remington; page 65, Custer's Hill drawing after a photograph by Barry; page 73, Taps by Remington, engraved by "S.C."; page 83, Cavalry Officer by Remington. The portraits of Terry (page 26), Sitting Bull (page 28), Crow King (page 29), and Gall (page 67) were drawn by Louise Pfeiffer. All of the other *marginalia* portraits are after photographs by Barry, except that of Lt. Sturgis (page 71) which is after a photograph by Pach.

COLOPHON

THIS VOLUME was designed by the publisher and made in San Francisco, California. The printing was executed by Jorgenson & Company, and the binding by Filmer Bros. - Taylor & Taylor. The typeface for the text and picture captions is Linotype Baskerville, composed by Timely Typography. The display types are Tuscan Outline and Modern No. 20, handset. The paper is Curtis Utopian and the cloth is Bancroft Natural Finish buckram.

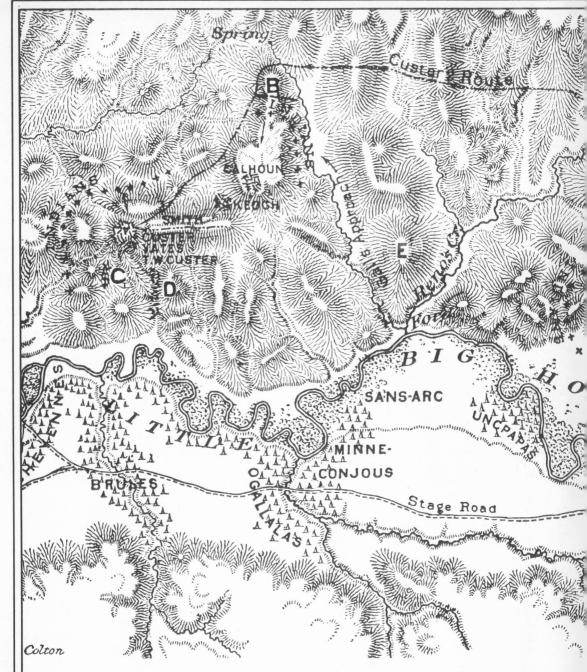

The TERRAIN of the BATT[LE]

A — Hill where Custer was seen by Reno's men during the fight in the valley, also the point reached by Reno's advance after the retreat from the valley, from which he fell back to the bluff where he was besieged. B — Where Keogh's and Calhoun's troops dismounted and advanced along the ridge to the point where their bodies were found. C — A few bodies found here, mostly from the commands of Yates and T. W. Custer, who for the greater part died with General